KEY FORESTS FOR THREATENED
BIRDS IN AFRICA

by

N. J. Collar and S. N. Stuart

in collaboration with the

IUCN Species Survival Commission

ICBP Monograph No. 3

Copyright © 1988 International Council for Bird Preservation.
32 Cambridge Road, Girton, Cambridge CB3 0PJ, U.K.

British Library Cataloguing in Publication Data

Collar, N. J. (Nigel James), *1946-*
  Key Forests for Threatened Birds in Africa
  1. Africa. Birds in danger of extinction
  I. Title II. Stuart, S. N. (Simon Nicholas)
  598'.042'096

ISBN 0-946888-15-9
ISSN 1012-6201

Printed and bound by S-Print, Cambridge.

INTERNATIONAL COUNCIL FOR BIRD PRESERVATION

ICBP is the longest-established worldwide conservation organisation. Its primary aim is the protection of wild birds and their habitats as a contribution to the preservation of biological diversity. Founded in 1922, it is a federation of 330 member organisations in 100 countries. These organisations represent a total of over ten million members all over the world.

Central to the successful execution of ICBP's mission is its global network of scientists and conservationists specialising in bird protection. This network enables it to gather and disseminate information, identify and enact priority projects, and promote and implement conservation measures. Today, ICBP's Conservation Programme includes some 100 projects throughout the world.

Birds are important indicators of a country's environmental health. ICBP provides expert advice to governments on bird conservation matters, management of nature reserves, and such issues as the control of trade in endangered species. Through interventions to governments on behalf of conservation issues ICBP can mobilise and bring to bear the force of international scientific and popular opinion at the highest levels. Conferences and symposia by its specialist groups help to attract worldwide attention to the plight of endangered birds.

ICBP maintains a comprehensive databank concerning the status of all the world's threatened birds and their habitats, from which the Bird Red Data Books are prepared. A series of Technical Publications gives up-to-date and in-depth treatment to major bird conservation issues. This series of Monographs (of which the present volume is the third) provides comprehensive, up-to-date information on specific or regional issues relating to bird conservation.

ICBP, 32 Cambridge Road, Girton, Cambridge CB3 0PJ, U.K.

U.K. Charity No. 286211

CONTENTS

ACKNOWLEDGEMENTS

Most of this text was prepared in mid-1985, when both of us worked at ICBP; later that year we were diverted from the project, and SNS joined the staff of IUCN. We were unable to resume and complete the work until late 1986 into 1987. We shall be very sorry if we fail here to thank anyone who helped us in the earlier phase of activity.

In particular, we owe R. J. Dowsett and F. Dowsett-Lemaire our warmest thanks for their exceptionally careful and very constructive review of the entire typescript (as it stood in April 1987), an act of kindness and goodwill which must have cost them many hours' work but which resulted in major improvements throughout the text. The following people very kindly commented on parts of the text in draft or otherwise provided information: J. S. Ash, T. M. Butynski, M. Carter, A. S. Cheke, G. R. Cunningham-van Someren, A. G. Davies, B. S. Decker, J. H. Fanshawe, J. S. Gartlan, W. Gatter, A. A. Green, K. Greer, G. E. Grout, J. A. Hart, J. F. M. Horne, P. C. Howard, K. M. Howell, B. Hughes, F. M. R. Hughes, B. J. Huntley, N. G. B. Johnston-Stewart, P. J. Jones, M. G. Kelsey, O. Langrand, M. Lawes, D. Lawson, M. Louette, J. C. Lovett, C. F. Mann, M. E. Nicoll, J. F. Oates, S. M. O'Connor, H. Oelke, A. Prigogine, W. von Richter, P. T. Robinson, L. L. Short, T. T. Struhsaker, C. A. Taylor, M. E. Taylor, P. B. Taylor, J. L. Tello, D. Thomas, R. du Toit, D. A. Turner, C. E. G. Tutin, J.-P. Vande weghe, J. Verschuren, S. M. Wells, R. Wilson, A. P. M. van der Zon.

At the IUCN Conservation Monitoring Centre, R. Madams, N. M. Collins and S. Davis kindly read all or part of the typescript and made valuable comments. In ICBP, Ch. Imboden, T. H. Johnson and S. M. Wells did likewise. We are also most grateful for help provided by T. J. Dee and A. J. Stattersfield at the ICBP Secretariat, and especially G. Pfaff who carefully wordprocessed a multitude of drafts, except for the penultimate two, which were ably done by I. Hughes. G. Pfaff also painstakingly prepared the disk for laser-printing. F. M. R. Hughes drew the maps: we thank her warmly. At the IUCN Species Survival Commission Executive Office, P. Chable, S. R. Edwards and N. Hennlich provided much-valued support, as did J. A. Sayer of the IUCN Tropical Forest Programme.

INTRODUCTION

In our recent study of threatened birds in Africa and its related islands (Collar and Stuart 1985; also Stuart and Collar in press) we identify 63 forest-dwelling or forest-associated bird species as at some risk of extinction on the African continent south of the Sahara, with a further 16 on Madagascar, seven on Mauritius, four on Grand Comoro (Comoro Islands), four on Mahé (Seychelles) and seven on São Tomé (São Tomé e Príncipe). In the individual accounts of these species we have endeavoured to spotlight the forests where more than one threatened bird occurs, since in the interests of economy it is important that "single species conservation" (action aimed at saving one species) wherever possible becomes rationalised as a component of "multiple species conservation" (which essentially means action to save an ecosystem). Here we move a stage further by establishing these forests as the units of concern, and offering what relevant supplementary data on them we can marshall from a survey necessarily limited by time.

Our definition of "threatened" (a general term we use to cover all "Red Data Book" species) is based entirely on our interpretation of IUCN criteria (see Collar and Stuart 1985: xxv-xxvi). In Appendices C and E of Collar and Stuart (1985) we make brief mention of (and define) "near-threatened species" and "incipient species at risk"; for the purposes of this analysis the latter are treated here as "near-threatened" (so also is the Congo Peacock *Afropavo congensis*, which we treat as Of Special Concern), and where appropriate we mention the presence of "near-threatened species" in the forests under review. Our definition of "forest" is essentially pragmatic. For the most part, the common assumption of a discrete wooded area in primary condition, surrounded by other vegetation types, applies; but in the case of West and parts of Central Africa and Madagascar the area of forest identified may form part of a wider block, and is differentiated only on the basis either of its likelihood of survival or, more rarely and less fairly, of its better ornithological coverage. In a few cases a group of small forests is treated as one. Our identification of a forest as important in the sense of our title results from its fulfilment of one of the following criteria:

(a) it holds more than one threatened bird species;
(b) it very probably holds more than one threatened bird species;
(c) it holds only one threatened species, but one which occurs nowhere else or only in one or a few much less significant (or less studied) localities;
(d) it holds one threatened and one or more near-threatened species.

In one case (Dja Game Reserve in Cameroon) we include a forest because we are confident it will prove to hold several threatened species although at present it remains ornithologically unsurveyed. In the case of Madagascar we have found it appropriate to drop some of the forest patches which would qualify for treatment under the criteria above, this action being explained in the introduction for that country. With these considerations, we identify a total of 75 forests as being important for threatened bird conservation in the area under review.

1

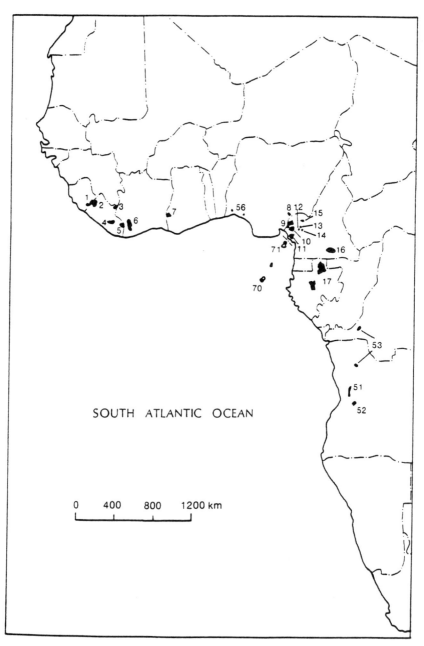

Map 1a: Forests in West Africa under review.

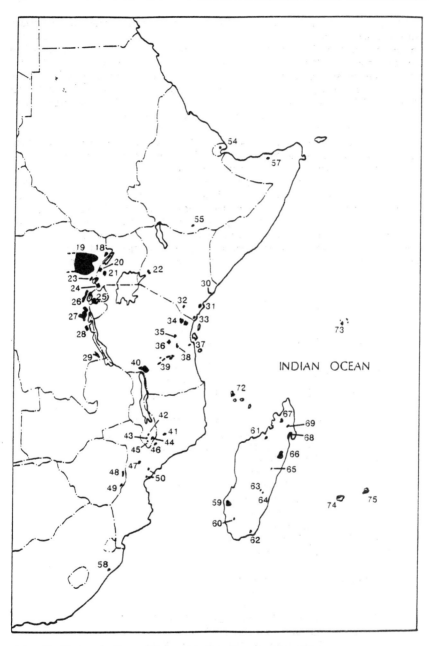

Map 1b: Forests in East Africa and Indian Ocean under review.

We have already indicated briefly that five main general regions in continental Africa emerge from our species-by-species analysis as critically important for threatened birds (Collar and Stuart 1985: xxviii). These are the Upper Guinea lowland rainforest block of West Africa; the montane and adjacent lowland forests of Cameroon and adjacent areas in Nigeria, Gabon and Equatorial Guinea (Western Refugium); the "Central Refugium" forests along and adjacent to the Albertine Rift; the East African coastal and montane relict forests extending south as far as the Eastern Highlands of Zimbabwe; and the forest patches of the Angolan escarpment. The individual forests or forest areas within these five regions that are important for threatened bird species are listed below, the letters a, b, c, d corresponding to the criteria for listing a forest described in the paragraph above, an asterisk (*) denoting a forest with more than two threatened bird species, and a question mark (?) indicating unproven qualification, while numbers correspond to those given in Maps 1a and 1b. In addition to the five main geographical regions in continental Africa referred to above, the remainder of Afrotropical Africa holds six important (in the sense of our title) forests, Madagascar nine and related islands six, and these are also listed below. Also in the table below, each forest is assigned a number, which is used throughout this document, and refers to the sequence in which the forests are discussed in the main text.

A.   *Upper Guinea* (west to east)
      1   a*   Gola Forest (Sierra Leone)
      2   b   Lofa-Mano proposed national park (Liberia)
      3   a*   Mount Nimba (Liberia)
      4   a*   Sapo National Park (Liberia)
      5   a*   Grand Gedeh County/Grebo National Forest (Liberia)
      6   a*   Tai National Park (Ivory Coast)
      7   b   Bia National Park (Ghana)

B.   *Cameroon (Western Refugium) forests* (west to east)
      8   a*   Obudu Plateau (Nigeria)
      9   a   Korup National Park and Mamfe region
      10   a*   Rumpi Hills
      11   a*   Mount Cameroon
      12   a*   Mount Kupe
      13   d   Mount Manenguba
      14   a*   Mount Nlonako
      15   a*   Mount Oku
      16   ?   Dja Game Reserve
      17   d   Forests in Gabon

C.   *Central Refugium* (north to south)
      18   a   Lendu Plateau (Zaïre)
      19   a*   Ituri Forest (Zaïre)
      20   d   Semliki (Bwamba) Forest (Uganda)
      21   c   Kibale Forest (Uganda)
      22   a   Kakamega and Nandi Forests (Kenya)
      23   a   Forest west of Lake Edward (Zaïre)
      24   a*   Impenetrable (Bwindi) Forest (Uganda)
      25   a*   Nyungwe (Rugege) Forest (Rwanda)

26 a   Forest west of Lake Kivu (Zaïre)
27 a*   Itombwe Mountains (Zaïre)
28 c   Mount Kabobo (Zaïre)
29 c   Marungu Highlands (Zaïre)

D. *East Africa* (north to south)
    30 a   Lower Tana riverine forests (Kenya)
    31 a*   Sokoke Forest (Kenya)
    32 c   Taita Hills (Kenya)
    33 a   Coastal forests in south-east Kenya
    34 a*   Usambara Mountains (Tanzania)
    35 d   Nguru Mountains (Tanzania)
    36 d   Ukaguru Mountains (Tanzania)
    37 a*   Pugu Hills (Tanzania)
    38 a*   Uluguru Mountains (Tanzania)
    39 a*   Uzungwa escarpment (Tanzania)
    40 d   Southern Highlands (Tanzania)
    41 a   Mount Namuli (Mozambique)
    42 a   Mount Chiradzulu (Malawi)
    43 a   Mount Soche (Malawi)
    44 a   Mount Mulanje (Malawi)
    45 a   Mount Thyolo (Malawi)
    46 d   Mount Chiperone (Mozambique)
    47 d   Gorongosa Mountain (Mozambique)
    48 d   Vumba Highlands (Zimbabwe and Mozambique)
    49 d   Chirinda Forest (Zimbabwe)
    50 d   Coastal forests in Sofala, Mozambique

E. *Angola scarp*
    51 a*   Amboim and adjacent forests, Gabela region
    52 d   Bailundu Highlands (Mount Moco)

F. *Africa: miscellaneous* (north to south)
    53 c   Forests of northern Angola and western Zaïre
    54 c   Day Forest (Djibouti)
    55 c   Forests around Neghelli (Ethiopia)
    56 c   Forests of south-western Nigeria
    57 c   Daloh Forest Reserve (Somalia)
    58 d   Ngoye Forest (South Africa)

G. *Madagascar* (west to east)
    59 a   Brush forest north of Tuléar
    60 a   Zombitse Forest
    61 a   Ankarafantsika Réserve Naturelle Intégrale
    62 d   Andohahela R.N.I. (Parcel 1)
    63 a*   Tsarafidy and Ankazomivady Forests
    64 a*   Ranomafana
    65 a*   Périnet-Analamazaotra Special Reserve
    66 a*   "Sihanaka Forest"
    67 a*   Tsaratanana Massif
    68 a*   Forests around Maroantsetra

69   a*   Marojejy Réserve Naturelle Intégrale and Andapa region

H.   *Islands* (west to east)
      70   a*   Forest in south-west São Tomé (São Tomé e Príncipe)
      71   c   Mount Malabo on Bioko (formerly Fernando Po) (Equatorial
                      Guinea)
      72   a*   Mount Karthala on Grand Comoro (Comoro Islands)
      73   a*   Central highland rainforest, Mahé (Seychelles)
      74   c   Plaine des Chicots, Réunion (to France)
      75   a*   Macchabé/Bel Ombre Nature Reserve (Mauritius)

From this list of islands we have excluded Praslin, Cousin and Frégate in the
Seychelles, and Rodrigues in the Mascarenes.   Praslin's forests hold Seychelles
Kestrels *Falco araea* and Seychelles Swiftlets *Collocalia elaphra*, plus the very
rare Seychelles Black Parrot *Coracopsis nigra barklyi*, but none of these qualifies
under our terms, the first being Out of Danger, the second being independent of
forest, and the third being a subspecies only.   Cousin holds the Seychelles
Warbler *Acrocephalus sechellensis* and Seychelles Fody *Foudia sechellarum*,
Frégate the Seychelles Magpie-robin *Copsychus sechellarum* and the Fody: but in
neither case does the woodland habitat comfortably match our notion of forest
(following, as we generally do here, the forest definitions of White 1983).   Both
the Rodrigues Warbler *Acrocephalus rodericanus* and Rodrigues Fody *Foudia
flavicans* were evidently once largely forest birds, but the tiny area in which they
now survive on the island consists of exotic secondary forest patches, plantations
and thicket, and is omitted here. Nevertheless, these island "forests" are important
to the conservation of the species in question, and would score 4, 9, 13 and 20
respectively under the system set out below, with the situation on Rodrigues
remaining critical.
    In the following documentation each of the eight groups above is treated
separately, and within these the important forests are listed in the order above,
with data arranged in standard sequence and, except for lesser known sites,
broken into three standard paragraphs.   The first gives its geographical coordinates
and general position, topography (including height above sea level) and geology,
broad vegetation-type with rainfall and temperature data where known, surface
area in square kilometres (sq km) and its official (legal) status.   The second lists
the threatened bird species present in the forest with the appropriate abbreviation
in parentheses after their scientific names signifying Red Data Book categories as
follows:

Endangered	E
Vulnerable	V
Indeterminate	I
Rare	R
Insufficiently Known	K
Out of Danger	O
Of Special Concern	OSC
Near-threatened	n-t

    Other threatened or otherwise noteworthy fauna and flora that a relatively
superficial reading of the literature shows to occur there are also mentioned in the
second paragraph, the categories of threat following those in IUCN/CMC (1986).

The third details the threats (if any) to the forest, and the conservation measures that are being or might or should be taken to protect it. References are provided for all this information save that concerning bird distribution, the sources for which are detailed fully in Collar and Stuart (1985); however, new data are referenced in the usual manner, although for various reasons it has not been possible to add the very few new data on distribution in the recent African update and global overview of Collar and Andrew (1988). Spellings of place names and coordinates are, where possible, taken from *The Times atlas of the world* (1986), and otherwise from Collar and Stuart (1985) or sources cited.

The introductory "Priorities for Conservation Action" is an attempt to rank the 75 forests in order of importance and urgency for conservation. As such, it should be compared with the emerging IUCN Species Survival Commission action plans which attempt a similar ranking process for other groups of species (e.g. Cumming and Jackson 1984, Oates 1986, East 1988), as well as with the priority assessments of MacKinnon and MacKinnon (1986).

It should be emphasised that the selection of forests for this review is based entirely on the criteria listed earlier in this Introduction. There are doubtless other forests which would qualify if we knew more of them. Nevertheless, always accepting the limitations imposed by ignorance, we feel that, in the continuing absence of full threatened species analysis for any other class of vertebrate, birds can serve – and be seen here to have done so – very effectively as practical first indicators of sites of general biological importance (notably in terms of endemism). As one of us (Collar 1987) has observed, the 75 forests reviewed in this study do not represent the minimum number that need conservation in Africa, but they are part of whatever that number may be.

PRIORITIES FOR CONSERVATION ACTION

In this section we attempt to identify the priorities for conservation action in terms of the bird species composition of these forests. A scoring system has been adopted which takes into account the Red Data Book categories of the species involved, as follows:

RDB Category	*Score*
Endangered (E)	5
Vulnerable (V)	4
Indeterminate (I)	4
Rare (R)	3
Insufficiently Known (K)	2
Out of Danger (O)	1
Of Special Concern (OSC)	1
Near-threatened (n-t)	1

If a species is endemic to a forest, or effectively so for practical conservation purposes, its score is doubled. Hence a forest with two endemic Endangered species scores 20. Forests which are poorly known ornithologically, but which almost certainly contain a number of rare bird species, have been scored as if the presence of these species has been confirmed (this principle has not been followed in the case of Madagascar, where our confidence of the likely distribution of birds is limited). Although this might lead to some inaccuracies, they seem likely to be fewer than if the species in question were excluded from the process. The results are given in Table 1 below.

No weighting is given to species with higher taxonomic distinctiveness, e.g. endemic genera or family, the chief effect of which would merely be to extend the lead of the island forests. No attempt is made to score the degree of threat to each forest, since this information was taken into account when assigning the RDB categories. Similarly the presence of other threatened fauna and flora in these areas is omitted from the scoring system since we lack the competence to undertake such an exercise. Some of these species will be covered in other conservation action plans being produced by the IUCN Species Survival Commission; meanwhile, we have at least done what we can to indicate the presence of threatened or endemic animals and plants in the individual forest accounts.

Table 1: Priority rating for forests important for threatened bird species conservation in the Afrotropical and Malagasy Region.

No.	Forest area	Priority score	Position
75	Macchabé/Bel Ombre Nature Reserve, Mauritius	64	1
70	Forests in south-west São Tomé	56	2
66	Sihanaka Forest, Madagascar	46	3
65	Périnet-Analamazaotra Faunal Reserve, Madagascar	44	4
27	Itombwe Mountains, Zaïre	40	5
31	Sokoke Forest, Kenya	34	6
19	Ituri Forest, Zaïre	31	7
34	Usambara Mountains, Tanzania	30	8
6	Tai National Park, Ivory Coast	29	9=
39	Uzungwa Mountains, Tanzania	29	9=
51	Amboim and adjacent forests, Angola	28	11=
15	Mount Oku, Cameroon	28	11=
5	Grand Gedeh County/Grebo National Forest, Liberia	27	13=
2	Lofa-Mano proposed national park, Liberia	27	13=
4	Sapo National Park, Liberia	27	13=
69	Marojejy R.N.I. and Andapa region, Madagascar	26	16=
64	Ranomafana	26	16=
3	Mount Nimba, Guinea, Liberia and Ivory Coast	26	16=
72	Mount Karthala, Comoro Islands	25	19=
68	Forest around Maroantsetra, Madagascar	25	19=
11	Mount Cameroon, Cameroon	23	21=
1	Gola Forest, Sierra Leone	23	21=
12	Mount Kupe, Cameroon	20	23=
38	Uluguru Mountains, Tanzania	20	23=
7	Bia National Park, Ghana	19	25
73	Mahé Highlands, Seychelles	17	26
26	Forest west of Lake Kivu, Zaïre	14	27
10	Rumpi Hills, Cameroon	13	28=
63	Tsarafidy and Ankazomivady Forests, Madagascar	13	28=
67	Tsaratanana Massif, Madagascar	13	28=
25	Nyungwe Forest, Rwanda	13	28=
59	Brush forest north of Tuléar, Madagascar	12	32=
8	Obudu Plateau, Nigeria	12	32=
37	Pugu Hills, Tanzania	12	32=
23	Forest west of Lake Edward, Zaïre	12	32=
14	Mount Nlonako, Cameroon	11	36

Table 1 contd

No.	Forest area	Priority score	Position
54	Day Forest, Djibouti	10	37=
30	Lower Tana riverine forests, Kenya	10	37=
45	Mount Thyolo, Malawi	10	37=
41	Mount Namuli, Mozambique	10	37=
56	Forests of south-western Nigeria	10	37=
18	Lendu Plateau, Zaïre	10	37=
29	Marungu Highlands, Zaïre	10	37=
32	Taita Hills, Kenya	9	44=
33	South-eastern coastal forests, Kenya	9	44=
42	Mount Chiradzulu, Malawi	9	44=
44	Mount Mulanje, Malawi	9	44=
43	Mount Soche, Malawi	9	44=
24	Impenetrable Forest, Uganda	9	44=
53	Forests of northern Angola and western Zaïre	8	50=
74	Plaine des Chicots, Réunion (France)	8	50=
61	Ankarafantsika R.N.I., Madagascar	8	50=
21	Kibale Forest, Uganda	8	50=
28	Mount Kabobo, Zaïre	8	50=
71	Mount Malabo, Equatorial Guinea	7	55
16	Dja Game Reserve, Cameroon	6	56=
55	Forests around Neghelli, Ethiopia	6	56=
22	Kakamega and Nandi Forests, Kenya	6	56=
60	Zombitse Forest, Madagascar	6	56=
50	Coastal forests in Sofala, Mozambique	6	56=
46	Mount Chiperone, Mozambique	6	56=
20	Semliki Forest, Uganda	6	56=
52	Bailundu Highlands, Angola	5	63=
9	Korup National Park, Cameroon	5	63=
13	Mount Manenguba, Cameroon	5	63=
62	Andohahela R.N.I., Madagascar	5	63=
58	Ngoye Forest, South Africa	5	63=
35	Nguru Mountains, Tanzania	5	63=
49	Chirinda Forest, Zimbabwe	5	63=
48	Vumba Highlands, Zimbabwe	5	63=
17	Forests in Gabon	4	71=
47	Gorongosa Mountain, Mozambique	4	71=
57	Daloh Forest, Somalia	4	71=
40	Southern Highlands, Tanzania	4	71=
36	Ukaguru Mountains, Tanzania	4	71=

This table gives a rough-and-ready picture of conservation priorities, from the viewpoint of the requirements of threatened bird species. It cannot pretend to inflexible authority, for at least five reasons.

1. Any scoring system (including the Red Data Book categories themselves) inevitably involves an element of subjectivity.

2. Certain high priority forest areas, such as those in Sierra Leone, Liberia, Ivory Coast and Ghana, have similar avifaunas. Another example is the Sihanaka Forest and Périnet-Analamazaotra Faunal Reserve in eastern Madagascar. The comprehensive safeguarding of a single large area might well be regarded as securing an entire region's avifauna, so that other areas sharing that avifauna would no longer rank as such serious contenders for immediate attention.

3. Any coherent conservation strategy needs to include areas like Mount Kabobo in Zaïre, Pico de Santa Isabel in Equatorial Guinea, and Daloh Forest in Somalia, which do not rank very high in this table, but which hold interesting rare species with very restricted distributions.

4. Decision-making will also include other species priorities, and other factors of conservation importance.

5. Basically, all 75 forests listed here are priorities, and all are important in that they have qualified for inclusion under the criteria listed in the Introduction. This list is the "Top 75" for birds out of a candidate list of hundreds around Africa.

Contemplation of Table 1 in the light of these cautionary remarks reveals one disturbing trend, namely that some forests of particularly high priority have been the focus of almost no conservation efforts. Examples include the forests of south-west São Tomé, Sihanaka Forest, Itombwe Mountains, Amboim and adjacent forests, and Grand Gedeh County and Grebo National Forest, although São Tomé is currently the subject of an ICBP project (Jones and Tye 1988).

UPPER GUINEA

The forests of Upper Guinea are those in West Africa, west of the so-called "Dahomey Gap" *(sensu* Moreau 1966) in Togo and Benin (Dahomey), and form part of the Guineo-Congolian regional centre of plant endemism as defined by White (1983). Substantial forest survives in five countries: Sierra Leone, Guinea, Liberia, Ivory Coast and Ghana. For the most part, this forest is at low altitudes, and even the higher peaks, such as Mount Nimba, lack a distinctive montane forest avifauna (Moreau 1966). The forest bird conservation problems and requirements have already been presented in a preliminary discussion by Thiollay (1985b). A number of endemic species occur in these forests, and these are often the most threatened today. Thiollay drew attention to the critical importance of the Tai National Park in Ivory Coast, and in the following pages we draw attention to six additional areas of importance. These areas are:

No.	Forest area	Priority score	Position among all the forests in this review
6	Tai National Park, Ivory Coast	29	9=
5	Grand Gedeh County/Grebo National forest, Liberia	27	13=
2	Lofa-Mano proposed national park, Liberia	27	13=
4	Sapo National Park, Liberia	27	13=
3	Mount Nimba, Guinea, Liberia and Ivory Coast	26	16=
1	Gola Forest, Sierra Leone	23	21=
7	Bia National Park, Ghana	19	25

- Details of the priority scores and how they are calculated are given in the introductory section "Priorities for Conservation Action". It will be noted that all seven of these areas score highly in Table 1 and this is because they contain the remnants of a very distinctive forest avifauna. It will also be noted from Map 2 that almost all these areas are crammed against their respective national boundaries, far from the national capitals. This partly reflects the extent to which development has driven nature to the farthest recesses of each country.

The Upper Guinea forest avifauna has not been well studied, and it is possible that further important areas will still be found, notably in Guinea, but also in Liberia and Ivory Coast (J. Verschuren *in litt.* 1986, H. H. Roth *in litt.* 1987). W. Gatter *(in litt.* 1987) considers that almost all forests in Liberia, if properly studied, would be found to qualify for inclusion in this publication under the criteria outlined in the Introduction, and the forested areas around Lamto in central-south Ivory Coast are known to have three threatened and four or five near-threatened forest bird species. Lamto has been omitted from this study because of its seeming unsuitability as a conservation area and the uncertainty of specific site data.   The other areas listed here are known to be of crucial importance, and all are in need of urgent conservation initiatives.

13

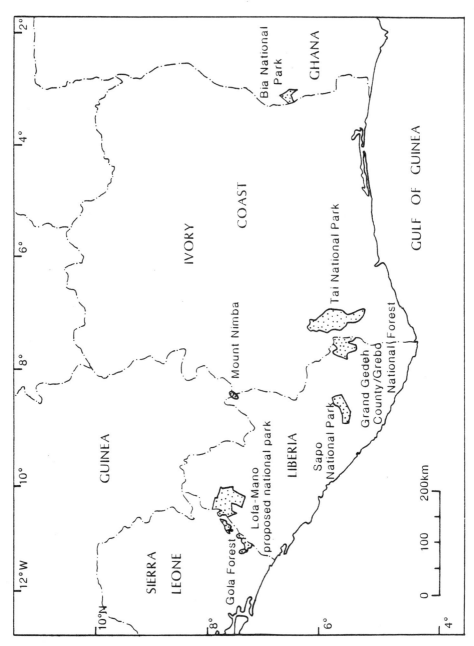

Map 2: **Upper Guinea**

1. Gola Forest   (Sierra Leone)   7°35'N 11°00'W

Situated in Kenema District, Eastern Province, adjacent to the border with Liberia, Gola Forest is divided into three forest reserves in two discrete blocks, Gola North and the contiguous Gola East and Gola West (Merz and Roth 1984, Davies 1987). Gola North is undulating or even mountainous terrain (highest point Sangie Mountain, 474 m), drained by the Moro and Mahoi Rivers; Gola East (drained by the Moro, Mano and Mahoi Rivers) and West (drained by the Mahoi and Moa Rivers) are relatively low-lying and flat, except for the northern hilly part of East (Merz and Roth 1984). The soil in Gola North is rich yellow-brown latosol, generally acidic (Cole 1980). Gola Forest chiefly consists of *Heritiera/Lophira* type tree formation, characterised by the predominance of *Heritiera utilis* and *Cryptosepalum tetraphyllum* in the main canopy, with *Erythrophleum ivorense* and *Lophira alata* and local concentrations of *Brachystegia leonensis* and *Didelotia idae*, the last being mutually exclusive of *Heritiera utilis*; the canopy is irregular, larger emergent trees reaching 50-55 m, general canopy height 30-35 m (Fox 1968, Davies 1987). Temperature is relatively constant throughout the year, around 29°C during the dry season (December to April) and 26°C during the rains (May to November); annual rainfall is 2,800 mm (Gola North) and 3,200 mm (Gola East) (Merz and Roth 1984). The forest covers 45,000 ha (North), 22,800 ha (East) and 6,200 ha (West); they have been Forest Reserves since 1926-1930 (Davies 1987).

The White-breasted Guineafowl *Agelastes meleagrides* (E), Western Wattled Cuckoo-shrike *Campephaga lobata* (V), Yellow-throated Olive Greenbul *Criniger olivaceus* (V) and Gola Malimbe *Malimbus ballmanni* (I), plus the near-threatened Rufous-winged Illadopsis *Trichastoma rufescens*, Black-headed Stream Warbler *Bathmocercus cerviniventris* and Copper-tailed Glossy Starling *Lamprotornis cupreicauda*, occur in Gola. In addition, the White-necked Picathartes *Picathartes gymnocephalus* (V) is confidently expected to occur since rocky outcrops are present, especially in Gola North, to provide suitable nest-sites (Davies 1987). The African Elephant *Loxodonta africana* (V), Chimpanzee *Pan troglodytes* (V) and Pygmy Hippopotamus *Choeropsis liberiensis* (V) are present in Gola, but confirmation is needed of the occurrence of Leopard *Panthera pardus* (V), Golden Cat *Felis auratus* and Jentink's Duiker *Cephalophus jentinki* (E) (Davies 1987). It is considered an important forest for primates (Oates 1986). The tree *Didelotia idae* is wholly endemic to Gola North and is one of an unspecified number of trees endemic to Gola Forest (Cole 1980, Davies 1987).

Gola Forest is principally threatened by logging: since at least the 1960s logging has been practised in varying degrees in all three forest reserves, and all three are currently part of Forest Industries Corporation timber concession (Tuboku-Metzger 1983, Merz and Roth 1984, Davies 1987). Relatively small areas (10 percent of Gola East, 3 percent of Gola North) would be inundated by the (currently shelved) Mano Hydroelectric Project (Merz and Roth 1984). In addition, commercial hunting by Liberians is extensive, causing disruption and imbalance (including the decline to extinction of some primates and ungulates), compounded by the use of the forest as smuggling routes (Davies 1987). Practical considerations have compelled conservationists to seek protection for Gola East over Gola North (Phillipson 1978, Merz 1986), but more recent analysis (Davies 1987) shows that highest conservation priority should go to Gola North, with the creation of a 20-40 sq km Strict Nature Reserve within a suggested Mogbai Conservation Area (= the entire Mogbai watershed, 55 sq km); the Wemago watershed area (in total 17 sq km) in northern Gola East also deserves

Conservation Area status, and Tiwai Island, 6 km upstream of Gola West, merits incorporation into the reserve system (Davies 1987). The foregoing proposals derive from a close perception of local realities; however, from both national and international perspectives, the Golas clearly merit complete protection as a national park, and indeed as a Biosphere Reserve as proposed by Cole (1980).

2. Lofa-Mano proposed national park (Liberia)   7°50'N 10°20'W
This area of forest lies in north-west Liberia against the frontier with Sierra Leone. There is no precise background information on the area but topography, geology and forest-type are all presumably fairly similar to those of the practically adjacent Gola Forest (q.v.) in Sierra Leone. The area of relatively untouched forest in north-west Liberia around 1980 was roughly 15,000 sq km and the Lofa-Mano forest as proposed for national park status covers about 2,300 sq km (Verschuren 1983). This latter area overlaps Gola National Forest and Kpelle National Forest, i.e. areas identified for timber extraction (Verschuren 1983).

The Yellow-throated Olive Greenbul *Criniger olivaceus* (V), Rufous-winged Illadopsis *Trichastoma rufescens* (n-t), Black-headed Stream Warbler *Bathmocercus cerviniventris* (n-t) and Copper-tailed Glossy Starling *Lamprotornis cupreocauda* (n-t) are known to occur in Lofa-Mano (W. Gatter *in litt.* 1987). There seems little doubt that when explored it will be found to hold an avifauna directly comparable to that in adjacent Gola Forest (Sierra Leone). Indeed there are records of White-necked Picathartes *Picathartes gymnocephalus* (V) and Rufous Fishing Owl *Scotopelia ussheri* (R) from Lofa County, the south-west of which falls within the Lofa-Mano delimitation (see maps in Verschuren 1983). In 1979, the fauna of Lofa-Mano was considered to be "certainly the most abundant in Liberia" (Verschuren 1983). Other species of very likely occurrence include the White-necked Guineafowl *Agelastes meleagrides* (E), Western Wattled Cuckoo-shrike *Campephaga lobata* (V) and Gola Malimbe *Malimbus ballmanni* (I). It is considered an important area for primate conservation (Oates 1986).

Present indications are that the Lofa-Mano National Park will not be gazetted, and so the future conservation of the area is in serious doubt (W. Gatter *in litt.* 1987). The proposed Mano dam along the Sierra Leone frontier will inundate a forest region "which is scenically and scientifically perhaps the most interesting and actually untouched landscape in Liberia" but at least the preservation of forest in Lofa-Mano above the dam will have the additional justification of water-catchment; the region is difficult of access and "practically uninhabited" (Verschuren 1983). Lofa-Mano has a very high score of 27 and ranks 13th= among the forests considered in this review.

3. Mount Nimba (Guinea, Ivory Coast and Liberia)   7°40'N 8°30'W
One of the greatest conservation causes and biological study areas in West Africa, Mount Nimba straddles the intersecting frontiers of three countries, Liberia, Guinea and Ivory Coast. The major cause of conservation concern has traditionally been in Liberia, although most of the surviving forest is in Guinea. The Nimba range is "a giant sheet of iron-containing quartzite" (Lamotte 1983), some 40 km long with a maximum width (in Guinea) of 12 km, and is generally oriented south-west/north-east (Coe and Curry-Lindahl 1965). At 550 m mean annual rainfall is about 2,000 mm, at the summit in Liberia (1,400 m) over 3,000 mm, and at these heights mean annual temperature is around 25°C and 20°C respectively; there is a main dry season from December to February and a main wet season from April to November, with a short dry period in July and August

at lower levels (Coe 1975, Colston and Curry-Lindahl 1986; also Coe and Curry-Lindahl 1965). Soils are generally deep, but poor on the light-coloured granites, more fertile on darker rocks (Lamotte 1983). Although Nimba's height (in the Liberian sector originally over 1,300 m, now owing to mining considerably lower) does not qualify the vegetation as montane, its habitat-types are quite distinct from those of the surrounding lowland forest, and it has the character of an inselberg: the lower slopes up to c.850 m consist of mixed rainforest (common genera being *Bussea, Chlorophora, Entandophragma, Lophira, Parkia, Piptadenia, Terminalia, Musanga, Harungana* and *Trema*) and above this level (which is the cloud-line) *Parinari excelsa* becomes dominant, forming a "mist" forest (Coe and Curry-Lindahl 1965, Colston and Curry-Lindahl 1986). Mount Nimba has experienced no official conservation in Liberia: two forest reserves in the 1970s covered 310 and 140 sq km each, but the area of mountain ceded to mining interests was 440 sq km (Coe 1975) and the rest merely under "symbolic protection" in the form of the Nimba Research Laboratory and global conservation opinion (Verschuren 1983). The Guinea and Ivory Coast sectors are inscribed on the World Heritage List (Lamotte 1983). The current protection of the remaining forests has become very critical. In Liberia all the forests, including those in the foothills, have been destroyed, except along the River Iti where protection is non-existent (J. Verschuren *in litt.* 1986). In Ivory Coast some relic forest patches survive (J. Verschuren *in litt.* 1986). The forest in Guinea is generally intact, although there is little foothill forest here, since the northern foothills are in the forest-savanna ecotone (J. Verschuren *in litt.* 1986).

The Rufous Fishing Owl *Scotopelia ussheri* (R), Yellow-footed Honeyguide *Melignomon eisentrauti* (K), Yellow-throated Olive Greenbul *Criniger olivaceus* (V), Western Wattled Cuckoo-shrike *Campephaga lobata* (V), White-necked Picathartes *Picathartes gymnocephalus* (V) and Nimba Flycatcher *Melaenornis annamarulae* (I) all occur on Mount Nimba (by mistake only three of these are listed for the locality in Collar and Stuart 1985: 332). The White-breasted Guineafowl *Agelastes meleagrides* (E) used to occur at Nimba, but has apparently been extirpated by man. Near-threatened species include Etchécopar's Barred Owlet *Glaucidium (capense) etchecopari*, Rufous-winged Illadopsis *Trichastoma rufescens*, White-eyed Prinia *Prinia leontica*, Black-headed Stream Warbler *Bathmocercus cerviniventris* and Copper-tailed Glossy Starling *Lamprotornis cupreocauda*. The Lesser Otter-shrew *Micropotomogale lamottei* – a monotypic genus – is known only from the mountain, and several other mammal species found there are rare elsewhere, including the bats *Myonycteris torquata leptodon, Scotonycteris zenkeri* and *S. ophiodon*, the Slender-tailed Squirrel *Allosciurus aubinii*, the Red-headed Forest Squirrel *Epixerus ebii jonesi*, and the Long-tailed Rat *Dephomys defua*. Leopards *Panthera pardus* (V) and Chimpanzees *Pan troglodytes* (V) are present, also (e.g.) the "rare" Johnstone's Genet *Genetta johnstoni* and African Golden Cat *Felis auratus* (Lamotte 1983). The viviparous toad *Nectophrynoides occidentalis* (V) – the only tailless amphibian in the world that is entirely viviparous – is known only from Nimba, and up to four other amphibians found there are very rare elsewhere (Coe 1975). Over 20 species of invertebrate are endemic to Mount Nimba (Lamotte 1983). Species diversity is very rich because of ecotone variety; over 500 new species of fauna have been described from the mountain (Lamotte 1983). Details of the vegetation are given by Adam (1966, 1970, 1971) and Jaeger and Adam (1975).

In 1955 Mount Nimba was discovered to possess massive deposits of high-grade iron-ore, and LAMCO (Liberian-American-Swedish Minerals Company) was formed to extract it: operations began in 1963 and continue today, coupled with the working of alluvial diamond deposits (Coe and Curry-Lindahl 1965, Coe 1975, Verschuren 1983). The resulting devastation of part of the mountain has been compounded by ill-considered dumping of capping waste, which has resulted in siltation of rivers and the death of riverine vegetation, and by the influx of probably over 20,000 people to the area, which has resulted in pressure on the land for farm use and on the fauna for bush-meat (Coe 1975). Timber concessions have been granted to NIMBACO (Verschuren 1983). Proposals for conservation at Nimba have repeatedly been made (Curry-Lindahl 1969, Coe 1975, Lamotte 1983, Verschuren 1983), and preservation of the forests on the mountain "is justified for pure economical reasons as essential water catchment areas" (Verschuren 1983; also Adam 1966, Lamotte 1983). In Liberia, urgent action is needed to protect the remaining forest along the River Iti (J. Verschuren *in litt.* 1986). The most important priority is to establish a protected area to conserve the remaining area of this unique forest in Guinea, which is already threatened by plans to extend the mining operations to that country (J. Verschuren *in litt.* 1986). Mount Nimba has a high score of 25 and ranks 16th= among the forests considered in this review.

4. Sapo National Park (Liberia)   5°30'N 8°40'W

This large lowland forest lies in ، the central part of south-east Liberia, and comprises the country's only national park. The topography is both hilly and flat, with much swampy habitat (Robinson and Peal 1981) and the elevation ranges from 120 to 360 m (M. Carter *in litt.* 1987). Although described simply as "primary rainforest" (Verschuren 1982), detailed surveys by botanists have shown the area to be 63 percent primary and mature secondary forest, 13 percent seasonally inundated forest, 13 percent swamp and 11 percent young secondary forest (Anderson *et al.* 1983). The surface area has been variously reported, most recently as 1,308 sq km (FDA/IUCN 1986). Annual rainfall ranges from 2,006 to 3,313 mm, decreasing to the north (M. Carter *in litt.* 1987). Temperatures vary from 22° to 28°C and humidity averages 91 percent (Anderson *et al.* 1983).

The White-breasted Guineafowl *Agelastes meleagrides* (E), Western Wattled Cuckoo-shrike *Campephaga lobata* (V), Yellow-throated Olive Greenbul *Criniger olivaceus* (V), White-necked Picathartes *Picathartes gymnocephalus* (V), Gola Malimbe *Malimbus ballmanni* (I), Rufous-winged Illadopsis *Trichastoma rufescens* (n-t), Black-headed Stream Warbler *Bathmocercus cerviniventris* (n-t) and Copper-tailed Glossy Starling *Lamprotornis cupreocauda* (n-t) have been recorded in Sapo (M. Carter *in litt.* 1987, W. Gatter *in litt.* 1987). The Rufous Fishing Owl *Scotopelia ussheri* (R), Yellow-footed Honeyguide *Melignomon eisentrauti* (K), Nimba Flycatcher *Melaenornis annamarulae* (I), and the very recently described and undoubtedly threatened Spot-winged Greenbul *Phyllastrephus leucolepis* (Gatter 1985) are also likely to occur; 114 bird species have been recorded to date (Carter 1987). Mammals present include Chimpanzee *Pan troglodytes* (V), *Colobus* monkeys, Elephant *Loxodonta africana* (V), Pygmy Hippopotamus *Choeropsis liberiensis* (V), Jentink's Duiker *Cephalophus jentinki* (E), Yellow-backed Duiker *C. sylvicultor*, Bongo *Tragelaphus eurycerus* and Leopard *Panthera pardus* (V) (Robinson 1982a,b, undated, Oates 1986). There is a chance that the extremely rare Liberian Mongoose *Liberiictis kuhni*, a monotypic genus, occurs in Sapo National Park (R. Wirth verbally 1986).

Until recently Sapo was completely divided into timber concession blocks and the success of the proposal to secure its future as a national park, considered vital (Robinson 1982a,b, undated), must now be followed by full support for its management plan (FDA/IUCN 1986). Sapo is surrounded by logging concessions and associated shifting agriculture; to date, attempts at encroachment by both loggers and cultivators have been effectively stopped by park staff (M. Carter *in litt.* 1987). Hunting still occurs in Sapo, primarily because there are no laws protecting wildlife in Liberia; the only legislation is a decree actually setting up the park (M. Carter *in litt.* 1987). Sapo National Park has a high score of 27, ranking 13th= among the forests considered in this review.

5. Grand Gedeh County/Grebo National Forest (Liberia) 5°45'N 7°35'W

Grand Gedeh County forms the easternmost part of the Liberian interior, and Grebo National Forest occupies a large proportion of the county (see map in Verschuren 1983). There is no precise background information on the area but topography, geology and forest-type are all presumably fairly similar to those of the practically adjacent Tai National Park (q.v.) in Ivory Coast. The area of Grebo National Forest was 2,510 sq km in 1978-1979 but most of it is under concession for timber extraction (Verschuren 1983). The easternmost part of these forests, along the border with Ivory Coast, now survives only as small patches, and protection for the whole area is non-existent (J. Verschuren *in litt.* 1986).

The White-breasted Guineafowl *Agelastes meleagrides* (E), Western Wattled Cuckoo-shrike *Campephaga lobata* (V), Yellow-throated Olive Greenbul *Criniger olivaceus* (V), White-necked Picathartes *Picathartes gymnocephalus* (V), Gola Malimbe *Malimbus ballmanni* (I) and the very recently described and undoubtedly threatened Spot-winged Greenbul *Phyllastrephus leucolepis* (Gatter 1985) have been recorded from forest in Grand Gedeh County. The Rufous Fishing Owl *Scotopelia ussheri* (R) is also likely to occur, and near-threatened species include the Rufous-winged Illadopsis *Trichastoma rufescens*, Black-headed Stream Warbler *Bathmocercus cerviniventris* and Copper-tailed Glossy Starling *Lamprotornis cupreocauda*. No precise inventory of mammals exists but it includes "elephants, hippo, buffaloes, many species of antelopes, leopards and many other animals" and the forest "is probably the area of Liberia which has the richest and best preserved animal life, because there are very few human inhabitants" (Curry-Lindahl 1969). Jentink's Duiker *Cephalophus jentinki* (E), Yellow-backed Duiker *C. sylvicultor* and Bongo *Tragelaphus eurycerus* occur (P. T. Robinson *in litt.* 1987). These forests constitute the only known locality of the extremely rare Liberian Mongoose *Liberiictis kuhni*, a monotypic genus, now considered as being in danger of extinction (R. Wirth verbally 1986).

The region is now largely parcelled out for logging, currently in operation, this development being "followed by the usual procession of shifting cultivators, hunting, etc.", and there is a proposed dam for the lower Cavally River which would affect the area (Verschuren 1983). This highly regrettable situation, given the patently remarkable diversity of rare species in the area, is marginally offset by the proposal (in Verschuren 1983) to establish a reserve in the Cavally valley at a site which takes in a small part of Grebo, is not directly threatened by concessions, and still holds "rather abundant" wildlife. If any other patches of non-threatened forest exist in the county, their wildlife value and conservation potential should be investigated. These forests have a very high score of 27 and rank 13th= among the forests considered in this review.

6. Tai National Park (Ivory Coast)   5°35'N 7°10'W

Tai forest lies between the Sassandra and Cavally Rivers (the former forming the boundary with deciduous forest, the latter forming the border with Liberia) in south-west Ivory Coast. The relief is flat in the north, hillier in the centre and south (up to 400 m), the surface largely granitic, soils mainly ferralitic or hydromorphic; the vegetation is dense lowland evergreen rainforest, rich in epiphytes and lianas and characterised by two aerial-rooted *Uapaca* spp. and with important trees such as *Coula*, *Garcinia*, *Allanblackia*, *Lophira*, *Tarrieta*, *Cynometra*, *Turreanthus*, *Entandrophragma*, *Mimusops* and *Piptadenia* (Rahm 1954, Guillaumet *et al.* 1984, Thiollay 1985a,b); Bousquet (1978) – see also FGU-Kronberg (1979) – distinguishes two major forest types, based on climatic and edaphic differences, that characterised by *Eremospatha macrocarpa* and *Diospyros manni* in the north and north-west, that by *Diospyros* spp. and *Mapania* spp. elsewhere (but reaching its fullest extent in the extreme south-west). Mean annual rainfall is 1,885 m (1,700 mm in the north-east, 2,200 mm in the south-west), with a dry season from mid-November to mid-March, temperatures always above 20°C and below 35°C, mean 25°C (Bousquet 1978, Collinet *et al.* 1984). The total area of the Tai complex (including buffer zones and game reserves) is 7,500 sq km, but the core protected area of national park is 3,500 sq km, one-third of which has been modified by illegal logging (Bousquet 1978, Roth 1985). The area has a long history of conservation prior to the establishment of the national park in 1972, and was declared a Biosphere Reserve in 1978 and included on the World Heritage List in 1982 (see Rahm 1973, Guillaumet 1976, Dosso *et al.* 1981, Roth 1985).

The White-breasted Guineafowl *Agelastes meleagrides* (E), Yellow-throated Olive Greenbul *Criniger olivaceus* (V), Western Wattled Cuckoo-shrike *Campephaga lobata* (V) and Nimba Flycatcher *Melaenornis annamarulae* (I) all occur in Tai, and it is very probable that the Rufous Fishing Owl *Scotopelia ussheri* (R) and Gola Malimbe *Malimbus ballmanni* (I) do also. Five near-threatened species, Etchécopar's Barred Owlet *Glaucidium (capense) etchecopari*, the Rufous-winged Illadopsis *Trichastoma rufescens*, White-eyed Prinia *Prinia leontica*, Black-headed Stream Warbler *Bathmocercus cerviniventris* and Copper-tailed Glossy Starling *Lamprotornis cupreocauda*, also occur. In addition, there is an apparently undescribed small oxpecker *Buphagus* that has been observed on Buffaloes *Syncerus caffer* inside Tai Forest (J.-M. Thiollay *in litt.* 1983; also Thiollay 1985a). Mammals present include Chimpanzee *Pan troglodytes* (V), Olive Colobus *Colobus verus*, Elephant *Loxodonta africana* (V), Pygmy Hippopotamus *Choeropsis liberiensis* (V) and Jentink's Duiker *Cephalophus jentinki* (E) (FGU-Kronberg 1979, Guillaumet and Boesch 1984, Oates 1986). There is a chance that the extremely rare Liberian Mongoose *Liberiictis kuhni*, a monotypic genus, occurs in Tai National Park (FGU-Kronberg 1979, R. Wirth verbally 1986). The park also holds over 80 plant species endemic to the Upper Guinea forests west of the Sassandra River (FGU-Kronberg 1979, Guillaumet and Boesch 1984; "over 150" such endemics claimed in Dosso *et al.* 1981), and its size is important for the survival of particularly rare species such as *Endotricha taiensis*, *Chrysophyllum letestuanum*, *Pancovia turbinata*, *Hirtella butayei*, *Kantou guereensis* (Bousquet 1978).

The Tai region of Ivory Coast was long a remote and sparsely peopled corner of the country, but in the 1960s the situation began to alter radically first with the economic development of the south-west (including the construction of major port facilities) and then, in the 1970s, with the resettlement there of large numbers of drought victims from the north (Rahm 1973, Halle 1983, Roth 1985). The park now suffers from timber extraction at the periphery, intrusion of agriculture within its borders, poaching and disturbance, e.g. from gold-prospectors (Bousquet 1978,

J.-M. Thiollay *in litt.* 1983). Stronger measures to provide effective management are clearly necessary for so crucial an area; these should include the promotion of tourism (FGU-Kronberg 1979). Tai National Park has a high score of 29 and ranks 9th= among the forests considered in this review.

7. Bia National Park (Ghana)   6°30'N 3°05'W

This park lies against the border with Ivory Coast in south-west Ghana, and embraces an extensive low undulating plateau (at 150-300 m) of middle-precambrian and granite rock with acrisol (forest ochrosol) soils ·(Taylor and Macdonald 1978, IUCN/UNEP 1987). The vegetation consists of both moist evergreen and moist semi-deciduous forest, dominated by species such as *Tieghemella heckelii, Entandrophragma angolense, Strombosia glaucocense* and the two palms *Raphia vinifera* and *R. gigantea* (IUCN/UNEP 1987). Temperatures range from 20°C to 34°C (IUCN/UNEP 1987). The total area is now 78 sq km, having originally (1974) been 306 sq km (Taylor and Macdonald 1978, IUCN/UNEP 1987); it is contiguous with the 225 sq km Bia Game Production Reserve, in which timber extraction is permitted and which grades into the evergreen forest zone (Hall and Swaine 1981, Gartlan 1982a). The forest is protected both as a national park and as a Biosphere Reserve.

The White-breasted Guineafowl *Agelastes meleagrides* (E) and Copper-tailed Glossy Starling *Lamprotornis cupreocauda* (n-t) have been recorded in Bia (Taylor and Macdonald 1978), and it seems very probable that several other threatened birds endemic to the Upper Guinea rainforest block, most likely the Yellow-throated Olive Greenbul *Criniger olivaceus* (V), Western Wattled Cuckoo-shrike *Campephaga lobata* (V) and Rufous Fishing Owl *Scotopelia ussheri* (R), will be found to occur there. Near-threatened species are likely to include the Rufous-winged Illadopsis *Trichastoma rufescens* and Black-headed Stream Warbler *Bathmocercus cerviniventris*. Mammals present include the Olive Colobus *Colobus verus*, Chimpanzee *Pan troglodytes* (V), Leopard *Panthera pardus* (V) and Elephant *Loxodonta africana* (V) (IUCN/UNEP 1987). It is considered an important forest for primate conservation (Oates 1986). Bia and Nini-Suhien (see below) are perhaps the only areas in Ghana where primary rainforest (0.6 percent of the country's original high forest) still exists (IUCN/UNEP 1987).

There are no immediate threats to the forest unless further reduction of the area under protection is contemplated (the forest is rich in valuable timber trees); however, poaching and tourist disturbance occur (IUCN/UNEP 1987). The opportunity for research as a means of demonstrating international interest has been emphasised by Gartlan (1982a).

Note added in proof   The likely importance of Nini-Suhien (Ghana) was missed by Collar and Stuart (1985) and only recognised when consulting Gartlan (1982a) for information on Bia for the present review.. In August/September 1988, at ICBP's suggestion, the Cambridge Ghana Rainforest Project surveyed Nini-Suhien and found White-breasted Guineafowl *Agelastes meleagrides* (E) and Copper-tailed Glossy Starling *Lamprotornis cupreocauda* (n-t), plus Diana Monkey *Cercopithecus diana* (V) (Mitchell 1988).

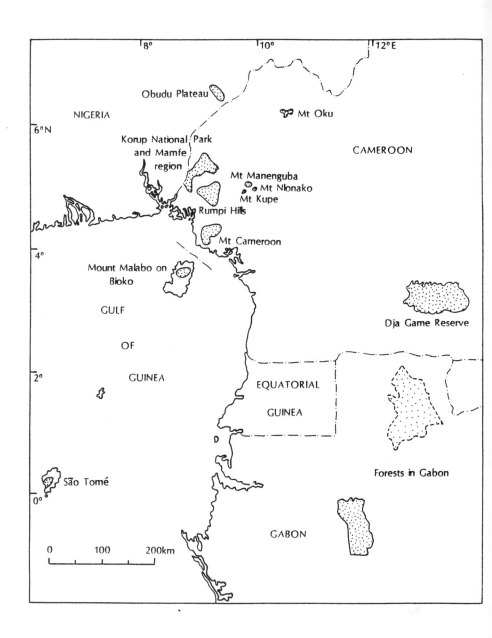

Map 3: Cameroon (Western Refugium) forests (with São Tomé)

22

CAMEROON (WESTERN REFUGIUM) FORESTS

The forests of the Western Refugium are centred on western and southern Cameroon, but also include adjacent areas of Nigeria, Gabon and Equatorial Guinea. The island of Bioko (formerly Fernando Po) also belongs here on biogeographic grounds, although in this review it is treated in the section on islands. The forest bird conservation problems have already been described in general terms by Thiollay (1985b) and a more detailed assessment of the problems and requirements in the montane areas is given in Stuart (1986a). In this review we identify ten forest areas of particular importance for forest bird conservation in the region:

No.	Forest area	Priority score	Position among all the forests in this review
15	Mount Oku, Cameroon	28	11=
11	Mount Cameroon, Cameroon	23	21=
12	Mount Kupe, Cameroon	20	23=
10	Rumpi Hills, Cameroon	13	28=
8	Obudu Plateau, Nigeria	12	32=
14	Mount Nlonako, Cameroon	11	36
16	Dja Game Reserve, Cameroon	6	56=
9	Korup National Park, Cameroon	5	63=
13	Mount Manenguba, Cameroon	5	63=
17	Forests in Gabon	4	71=

Details of the priority scores and how they are calculated are given in the introductory section "Priorities for Conservation Action". It will be noted that for birds the montane areas tend to score more highly than the lowland forests. This is the opposite of the situation for primates (see Oates 1986). Map 3 shows the geographic locations of these ten key conservation areas.

The forest avifauna of the Western Refugium has been better studied than that in Upper Guinea, but nevertheless it is still likely that other important areas will be found, especially in south-eastern Nigeria, Gabon and Rio Muni (the mainland part of Equatorial Guinea). Nevertheless, Mounts Oku and Cameroon in particular will always be unique areas of great importance for conservation.

8. Obudu Plateau (Nigeria)   6°30'N 9°15'E

This small montane area lies in south-east Nigeria north of Cross River and close to the border with Cameroon (and is essentially a western outlier of the mountain chain of south-west Cameroon). The general elevation is 1,500 m, with a few summits rising almost to 2,000 m, the plateau deeply dissected; most of the area, though originally forested, is now grassland, with forest confined to steep-sided valleys and scarps (Hall 1981). The forest flora is an attenuated variant of the endemic-rich lowland forest of the adjacent Oban region (south of Cross River), enriched with species of Afromontane affinity (Hall 1981). Mean annual rainfall is high, at least 4,280 mm, falling mainly in a nine-month rainy season (the plateau's ferralitic soils reflect the intense leaching that results), and temperatures are low, with monthly means of 14-16°C (daily minima) and 18-25°C (daily maxima) (Hall 1981). The whole area of the Obudu Plateau is 720 sq km, but the forest within it covers a very much smaller area (IUCN/UNEP 1987). Three forest reserves, together covering 720 sq km, were gazetted in 1933 and have been integrated to form a proposed game reserve, though the area has yet to be formally gazetted (IUCN/UNEP 1987).

The Green-breasted Bush-shrike *Malaconotus gladiator* (R), White-throated Mountain Babbler *Lioptilus gilberti* (R), Bannerman's Weaver *Ploceus bannermani* (V), Cameroon Mountain Greenbul *Andropadus montanus* (n-t), Grey-headed Greenbul *Phyllastrephus poliocephalus* (n-t) and, possibly, the Cameroon Mountain Roughwing *Psalidoprocne fuliginosa* (n-t) occur on the Obudu Plateau. The Fernando Po Swift *Apus sladeniae* (K), probably not a forest-dependent species, has also been recorded. It is considered an important area for primate conservation (Oates 1986). In addition, a frog *Cardioglossa schioetzi* is known only from Obudu and the nearby Oshie area in Cameroon (Gartshore 1986). The vegetation of the region is of considerable interest, and a cline of unbroken, little disturbed high forest stretches from the Oban lowlands in the south to the plateau's peaks over an altitudinal range of nearly 2,000 m (a situation rare in Africa) (Hall 1981). Forty-two of Nigeria's 550 threatened plant species are recorded for the Obudu Plateau (Gbile *et al.* 1978).

Habitat degradation on Obudu is currently resulting from excessive grazing and uncontrolled movement of cattle (causing erosion), clearance of forest for firewood and building material, and inappropriate burning; consequently "the economic value of the area as range will inevitably suffer and the potential of the Plateau as a tourist resort and beauty spot ... is likely to decline. Also ... watershed protection ... would be rendered less effective" (Hall 1981). In recent years the situation has markedly deteriorated, partly owing to a large influx of squatters (Ash and Sharland 1986). Farming needs to be confined to areas of relatively level grassland and a rotational system adopted to maintain crop-growth capacity, small *Eucalyptus* plantations could provide local needs for wood, other plantation work could control erosion, and burning should be controlled or eliminated (Hall 1981). Indeed, the great ecological interest of the ecotone, the rarity of comparable phenomena in Africa, and the floristic endemism involved, combine to suggest that the whole Oban/Obudu region over a distance of some 100 km might best be conserved as a national park (Hall 1981); this view is endorsed and expanded by Ash and Sharland (1986), who argue that amalgamation of the Obudu Forest Reserve with the Boshi-Okwango Forest Reserves in a national park is worthy of immediate implementation.

9. Korup National Park and Mamfe region (Cameroon) 5°20'N 9°30'E

Korup lies against the Nigeria border in westernmost Cameroon, the Mamfe region being just to the north of the park boundaries. The relief is low and flat in the south with an increase in inselbergs, rocks and ancient volcanic extrusions towards the centre and north, the highest point being Yuhan hill at 1,079 m; the basement rock is of precambrian age but several volcanic episodes have occurred, the soils being rather acid, nutrient-poor and sandy, derived from quartz and granite (Gartlan and Agland 1981). The vegetation in the reserve (and presumably therefore to the north of it) is low-elevation, dense, humid evergreen forest of the Biafran type; mean annual rainfall is around 6,000 mm, rainfall increasing from the dry months of December and January towards August, September and October, the wettest months (Gartlan and Agland 1981). The area of the national park is 837 sq km (IUCN/UNEP 1987).

The Grey-necked Picathartes *Picathartes oreas* (R) is recorded from both Korup National Park and around Mamfe; the Yellow-footed Honeyguide *Melignomon eisentrauti* (K) is recorded from around Mamfe. Seven threatened mammals occur in Korup, the Collared Mangabey *Cercocebus torquatus* (V), Russet-eared Guenon *Cercopithecus erythrotis* (V), Preuss's Guenon *C. preussi* (V), Drill *Papio leucophaeus* (E), Preuss's Red Colobus *Colobus badius preussi* (E), Elephant *Loxodonta africana* (V) and Leopard *Panthera pardus* (V) (Gartlan and Agland 1981, Gartlan 1986). It is considered one of the most important areas for primate conservation in Africa (Oates 1986). Two very scarce species of toad occur, *Bufo superciliaris* and *Nectophryne afra* (Gartlan 1986). Tree species inventory work had by 1981 revealed 17 previously undescribed species and possibly two new genera, and the plant diversity of Korup was considered comparable to that recorded in any African forest (Gartlan and Agland 1981). Korup is a centre of endemism with many narrowly endemic plant species, e.g. *Hymenostegia bakeriana*, *Globulostylis talbotii*, *Soyauxia talbotii*, *Deinbollia angustifolia*, *Camplyospermum dusenii*, *Deinbollia saligna*, *Eugenia dusenii*, *Medusandra richardsiana*, *Ouratea dusenii* and *Phyllanthus dusenii*; possibly as many as 5 percent of the tree species of Korup may be narrowly endemic (Gartlan 1986, Thomas 1986b).

The forest is not yet seriously threatened, the region being remote and typical timber trees being so scarce that the forest has almost no commercial value (Gartlan and Agland 1981); however, since May 1986 a new road has allowed access at all seasons (Cloutier and Dufresne 1986).

10. Rumpi Hills (Cameroon) 4°50'N 9°06'E

These lie north-north-west of Mount Cameroon and well west of Mount Kupe, forming an extensive area of relatively low, undulating hills with a few peaks above 1,000 m (the highest being Mount Rata at 1,768 m), and with many permanent watercourses which affect the character of the forest (Tye 1986). The forest is very wet, its total area is unknown although the hills are approximately 45 x 30 km (i.e. 1,350 sq km), and much of it is within forest reserves (Tye 1986). Montane plant species, such as *Xylopia africana*, are restricted to the mountain summits (Thomas 1986a).

Three threatened birds, the Green-breasted Bush-shrike *Malaconotus gladiator* (R), White-throated Mountain Babbler *Lioptilus gilberti* (R) and Grey-necked Picathartes *Picathartes oreas* (R), and four near-threatened birds, the White-naped Pigeon *Columba albinucha*, Cameroon Mountain Greenbul *Andropadus montanus*, Grey-headed Greenbul *Phyllastrephus poliocephalus* and Ursula's Mouse-coloured Sunbird *Nectarinia ursulae*, occur in the Rumpi Hills. Two rare primates, the Russet-eared Guenon *Cercopithecus erythrotis* (V) and Preuss's Guenon *C. preussi* (V), also occur (Bowden 1986b). The chameleon *Chamaeleo eisentrauti* is known only from the Rumpi Hills, and the toad *Werneria tandyi* is otherwise known only from Mount Manenguba (Gartshore 1986).

The forests of the Rumpi Hills are relatively well preserved at present: the area is remote and there are few roads, while cutting takes place only around villages (Stuart 1986a). If the area is to be opened up for economic development, this should be planned carefully with an integrated land-use and management plan, which includes adequate measures for the conservation of water catchments, timber resources and biological diversity (Stuart 1986a).

11. Mount Cameroon (Cameroon)   4°13'N 9°11'E
This large, isolated mountain lies next to the sea in south-west Cameroon. It is 50 x 35 km in dimensions and reaches 4,005 m: it is the highest mountain as well as the only active volcano in West Africa, but possesses no main crater, eruptions occurring through fissures (Tye 1986). Forest extends from sea-level (but is now cleared from the coast) up to 2,000 to 2,500 (generally c.2,100) m, and thus ranges from lowland rainforest to high montane forest, much of the upper forest being a patchwork of regenerating areas owing to lava flows (Thomas 1986a). The total area of forest is unknown but merely by superimposing a rectangle that can hold within it the 1,000 m contour, and which by chance is a simple 40 x 20 km, an extremely approximate figure of 800 sq km can be derived, perhaps up to 1,000 sq km if allowance for elevation is made. The Bambuko Forest Reserve covers the north-west quarter of the mountain (from the peak north and west very roughly to the 500 m contour) and from very crude measurement on a map might cover some 300 sq km; otherwise the mountain and its forests receive no protection. The forest flora is very diverse, and the communities are described and some of the more important species listed by Thomas (1986a) and also Baker (1986).

The Mount Cameroon Francolin *Francolinus camerunensis* (R) is entirely restricted to forest on Mount Cameroon. Two other threatened birds, the Green-breasted Bush-shrike *Malaconotus gladiator* (R) and Grey-necked Picathartes *Picathartes oreas* (R), also occur there, and a fourth, Bates's Weaver *Ploceus batesi* (R), has been recorded in forest at the southern foot of the mountain; a fifth, Monteiro's Bush-shrike *M. monteiri* (I), has been recorded once (in the last century), but is otherwise restricted to the scarp of Angola (including Amboim forest, etc., q.v.). It should also be pointed out that the Yellow-footed Honeyguide *Melignomon eisentrauti* (K) is known from Malende, not far from the north-eastern foot of the mountain. Four near-threatened birds, the Cameroon Mountain Roughwing *Psalidoprocne fuliginosa*, Cameroon Mountain Greenbul *Andropadus montanus*, Grey-headed Greenbul *Phyllastrephus poliocephalus* and Ursula's Mouse-coloured Sunbird *Nectarinia ursulae*, also occur on Mount Cameroon. It is an important locality for the Russet-eared Guenon *Cercopithecus erythrotis* (V) and Preuss's Guenon *C. preussi* (V) (Bowden 1986b). Other species for which Mount Cameroon is important are the skink *Panaspis gemmiventris* (otherwise known only from Bioko), two toads *Didynamipus sjoestedti* and *Werneria preussi*, and a very rare treefrog *Hyperolius krebsi* (Gartshore 1986). For no fewer than 51 of the 111 plant species in need of protection in Cameroon, Mount Cameroon is indicated as the principal if not the only locality (Hazlewood and Stotz 1981), but it is not clear if these are all endemic to Cameroon or are forest or non-forest species: for instance, Mount Cameroon is known to be important for endemic grasses (A. P. M. van der Zon *in litt.* 1987), but many of these are presumably non-forest species. According to Brenan (1978), 45 plants appear to be endemic to Mount Cameroon.

The south-east and south sides of the mountain are well populated and thus vulnerable to deforestation: the area above and below Buea is cut over by local people (Stuart 1986a) and plantations of oil-palms are likely to be extended along the coast and inland (M. C. Hodgson verbally 1983). Cutting of trees is taking place in the foothills on all slopes of the mountain, including the Bambuko Forest Reserve in which such activities are illegal (Stuart 1986a). Hunting pressure is also severe (Stuart 1986a). A national park has been recommended for Mount Cameroon for its recreational, touristic and educational value (Dufresne and Cloutier 1982); national park status for the mountain is also to be urged for its major biological value (Stuart 1986a). Such a park should comprise the southern slopes bordering the sea, including the lowland rainforest, as well as the existing Bambuko Forest Reserve on the north-western slopes; the establishment of this park would require the cancellation of timber and agricultural concessions on the southern slopes, but otherwise no great economic sacrifice would be required (SNS). Mount Cameroon has a high score of 23 and ranks 20th= among the forests considered in this review.

12. Mount Kupe (Cameroon)   4°48'N 9°42'E
In the south-west/north-east running mountain chain that dominates south-west Cameroon, Mount Kupe is the first major peak inland from Mount Cameroon. Nevertheless it is much smaller and only half as high as the latter: moreover, it is not volcanic but consists of a massive horst (of granite and syenite) formed by blockfaulting and bounded by structural troughs (Tye 1986). The vegetation is closed-canopy rainforest, 10-15 m in height (Baker 1986), arising from a "sea" of farm-bush and banana plantations, and is estimated to cover only c.21 sq km (Hall and Moreau 1962) – recent experience of the site suggests this figure is probably accurate (SNS). Montane species of plant, such as *Podocarpus latifolius* and *Philippia mannii*, are apparently restricted to the mountain summit (Thomas 1986a); *Carapa* sp., *Cephaelis mannii*, *Dicranolepis vestita* and *Ficus mucuso* are "noted" trees, with *Dorstenia*, *Dracaena*, *Haemanthus*, *Selaginella vogelii* and many ferns present both on the ground and as epiphytes (Baker 1986). Mount Kupe is unprotected except by a local tribal taboo.
    The Mount Kupe Bush-shrike *Malaconotus kupeensis* (I) is entirely restricted to forest on Mount Kupe. Three other threatened birds, the Green-breasted Bush-shrike *Malaconotus gladiator* (R), White-throated Mountain Babbler *Lioptilus gilberti* (R) and the Grey-necked Picathartes *Picathartes oreas* (R), also occur there, as do three near-threatened birds, the Cameroon Mountain Greenbul *Andropadus montanus*, Grey-headed Greenbul *Phyllastrephus poliocephalus* and Ursula's Mouse-coloured Sunbird *Nectarina ursulae*. The Fernando Po Swift *Apus sladeniae* (K), probably a non-forest species, has been recorded from Bakossi, near Mount Kupe. Two threatened species of primate occur on Mount Kupe, the Russet-eared Guenon *Cercopithecus erythrotis* (V) and the Drill *Papio leucophaeus* (E) (Bowden 1986b). The skink *Panaspis pauliani* occurs on Kupe and is otherwise known only from the Bamboutos Mountains (Gartshore 1986). Although Hazlewood and Stotz (1981) misclass the forest on Kupe, they indicate that for no fewer than 15 of the plant species in need of protection in Cameroon Mount Kupe is apparently the principal if not the only locality, these being *Glossocalyx brevipes*, *Pentabrachium reticulatum*, *Hamilcoa zenkeri*, *Eurypetalum unijugum*, *Medusandra richardsiana*, *Calochone acuminata*, *Atractogyne gabonii*, *Dielsantha galeopsoides*, *Didymocarpus kamerunensis*, *Whitfieldia preussi*, *Filetia africana*, *Afrofittonia silvestris*, *Barombia gracillima*, *Guaduella ledermannii*, *Puelia acuminata*.
    Tree-cutting is taking place around the base of Mount Kupe, which stands in an area of dense human population (Stuart 1986a). The area is so small that it is permanently vulnerable to exploitation, and the taboo that currently protects it is

presumably liable to breakdown at any time. In view of the area's uniqueness, national park status is merited (Stuart 1986a).

13. Mount Manenguba (Cameroon)   5°01'N 9°51'E
This mountain lies to the north and slightly east of Mount Kupe, but is far larger and somewhat higher (2,411 m). It is an extinct volcano with a caldera 4 km in diameter, containing two crater lakes (Tye 1986). The forest is stunted, dry and montane in character, possibly as a consequence of being in Mount Kupe's rain-shadow; it is also both patchy and scrappy, owing to much cutting, burning and grazing, and probably now covers less than 10 sq km, most of the mountain being covered in short grassland (Thomas 1986a). The plant species are similar to those at equivalent elevations on Mount Cameroon (Thomas 1986a) though the abundance of *Polyscias fulva* gives the vegetation a very different appearance.

Bannerman's Weaver *Ploceus bannermani* (V) and the Cameroon Mountain Greenbul *Andropadus montanus* (n-t) occur in the forest on Mount Manenguba. Hartwig's Soft-furred Rat *Praomys hartwigi* and the shrew *Silvisorex granti camerunensis* occur elsewhere only on Mount Oku (q.v.) (Bowden 1986a, Macleod 1987). The chameleon *Chamaeleo q. quadricornis* is endemic to Manenguba, as are five species of frog, *Cardioglossa trifasciata, Leptodactylon erythrogaster, Phrynodon* sp., *Leptopelis* sp. and *Astylosternus* sp. (these last three await description) (Gartshore 1986). Also, two toads are almost restricted to Manenguba, these being *Werneria tandyi* (otherwise found only in the Rumpi Hills) and *W. bambutensis* (also known from the Bamboutos Mountains) (Gartshore 1986).

The remaining forest on Manenguba is steadily diminishing through human agency. The north-west sector, where a road runs from Bangem to the crater, is entirely cleared. The crater is spectacularly beautiful and a worthy tourist attraction: conservation needs to be structured into tourist development, with appropriate tree plantations buffering the remaining forest patches (Stuart 1986a). A land-use plan which addresses the problems of overgrazing, fire, wood supplies, water catchments, biological diversity and tourism is urgently needed (Stuart 1986a) and should be undertaken by an aid agency.

14. Mount Nlonako (Cameroon)   4°53'N 9°55'E
A sister mountain in size and type to Mount Kupe, Nlonako lies just south-east of Mount Manenguba. It is part of an uplifted mass of precambrian granite and gneiss, rising to 1,825 m (Tye 1986). The vegetation is closed canopy tall montane forest, and probably covers not more than 20 sq km (SNS).

Three threatened birds, the Green-breasted Bush-shrike *Malaconotus gladiator* (R), White-throated Mountain Babbler *Lioptilus gilberti* (R) and Grey-necked Picathartes *Picathartes oreas* (R), and two near-threatened birds, the Grey-headed Greenbul *Phyllastrephus poliocephalus* and Ursula's Mouse-coloured Sunbird *Nectarinia ursulae*, occur on Mount Nlonako. Collar and Stuart (1985:715) listed the Cameroon Mountain Greenbul *Andropadus montanus* from Mount Nlonako in error.

Deforestation has occurred on the north-west side of the mountain from the town of Nkongsamba to the peak, but much of the forest is protected by the rugged terrain (Stuart 1986a). More surveys are needed to assess the biological importance of Mount Nlonako. The area probably deserves some formal conservation status and measures should be taken to restrict the expansion of the farmed areas on the north-western slopes (Stuart 1986a).

Cameroon (Western Refugium) 29

15. Mount Oku (Cameroon) 6°12'N 10°32'E

Mount Oku dominates the northern part of the Bamenda Highlands. At 3,011 m
it is the second highest mountain in West Africa and was formed by a
combination of uplifting and volcanic action, but as it is much older than Mount
Cameroon it possesses a mature, rounded relief with steep, dissected slopes and
much surface drainage; on its western flank lies Lake Oku, a crater lake at
2,227 m surrounded by primary montane forest (Tye 1986, Numbem 1987, Wilson
1987). Soils are ferralitic, acid and low in nutrients, well drained with a high clay
content; most rain falls between July and September, with probably over
3,000 mm per year at the summit and around 2,000 mm per year lower on the
mountain, where temperatures vary seasonally between means of 13° and 22°C
(9-19°C at the summit) (Numbem 1987). Forest on Mount Oku extends from
2,100 m up to the summit plateau but, because of degradation through grazing
and burning, the vegetation consists of moist montane forest, degraded montane
forest, bamboo *Arundinaria alpina*, scrublands/tree savanna, and grassland; the
primary montane forest has a low canopy (10-20 m) with occasional trees up to
30 m, rich in epiphytes though poor in lianas (Thomas 1987). At lower levels
the forest is dominated by *Schefflera abyssinica* and *Carapa grandiflora*, while at
higher elevations the canopy is dominated by *Syzygium staudtii*, *Rapanea
neurophylla* and *Podocarpus latifolius*, the last on steep ridges (Thomas 1987).
Important trees at 2,300 m near Lake Oku include *Agauria*, *Ixora*, *Myrica*, *Nuxia*,
Polyscias, *Schefflera* and *Syzygium*; above 2,600 m, bamboo *Arundinaria*,
Podocarpus, *Philippia*, *Myrica* and *Lasiosiphon* are dominant (Thomas 1986a).
The combined area of primary and degraded forest is 6,900 ha; prefectural orders
provide slender protection (Macleod 1987).

Bannerman's Turaco *Tauraco bannermani* (E) and the Banded Wattle-eye
Platysteira laticincta (E), though endemic to the whole Bamenda Highlands, find
their best refuge and only hope for survival in the forests of Mount Oku. Two
other threatened birds, the Green-breasted Bush-shrike *Malaconotus gladiator* (R)
and Bannerman's Weaver *Ploceus bannermani* (V), and the near-threatened
Cameroon Mountain Greenbul *Andropadus montanus*, also occur on Oku. The
forest holds an important population of Preuss's Guenon *Cercopithecus preussi*
(V), and Hartwig's Soft-furred Rat *Praomys hartwigi* and the shrew *Silvisorex
granti camerunensis* occur elsewhere only on Mount Manenguba (Bowden 1986a).
Mount Oku has an important population of Cooper's Green Squirrel *Aethosciurus
cooperi* (Bowden 1986a) and several rare amphibians also occur, including an
undescribed clawed toad *Xenopus* sp., probably endemic to Lake Oku, a toad
Wolsterstorffina mirei (otherwise known only from the Bamboutos Mountains),
and a frog *Astylosternus ranoides* (known also from Mount Neshele and the
Bamboutos Mountains) (Gartshore 1986). Another frog, *Leptodactylon axillaris*,
known only from the Bamboutos Mountains, almost certainly occurs on Mount
Oku (Gartshore 1986). One orchid, *Disperis nitida*, is endemic to the mountain
and a few nearby sites (Macleod 1987, Thomas 1987). The highest part of the
forest (from the summit for 300-400 m) is dominated by *Podocarpus*/bamboo, a
unique formation in West Africa (Macleod 1987).

The forest on Oku is very seriously threatened by agricultural encroachment,
illegal grazing, fire damage and over-exploitation of *Pygaeum* bark; as recently as
1963 forest covered 17,500 ha, this reducing to 8,700 ha by 1983, with 1,700 ha
of this being lost and another 2,700 ha badly damaged by 1986 (Macleod 1987).
The remaining forest area should become a Protection Forest, all encroachment

and degradation by farming, grazing and burning should cease (although sustainable forest-based activities may continue), a reafforestation and regeneration programme is needed, faunal and floral inventories should be completed, conservation education and extension is necessary, tourism needs careful integration, and a regional programme of land-use development is required; long-term technical assistance should be provided to accomplish these recommendations (Macleod 1987). These recommendations are being followed through in an ICBP project supported by WWF-US and the U.K. Overseas Development Administration (*ICBP XX Bull.*, 1988; M. R. W. Rands verbally 1988). Mount Oku represents the most biologically differentiated and most seriously threatened of all the forests in the Western Refugium, has a very high score of 28 and ranks 10th= among the forests considered in this review.

16. Dja Game Reserve (Cameroon)   3°00'N 13°00'E
This lowland site lies in a large meander of the River Dja in the central part of southern Cameroon. The elevation is between 600 and 900 m, the relief fairly flat except in the south-east where tributaries of the Dja have cut deep beds; most of the reserve lies on middle to late precambrian rocks, chiefly schists and gneisses, and the soils are red and ferralitic (Gartlan and Agland 1981). There are four basic habitat-types in the reserve, these being (a) uncut high forest, (b) swamp vegetation, (c) old secondary forest and (d) recently abandoned cocoa and coffee plantations (Gartlan and Agland 1981). The chief habitat is thus medium-altitude humid evergreen forest of the Congolese type, and the area of the reserve is 5,400 sq km (Gartlan and Agland 1981). The reserve is already a Strict Nature Reserve and Biosphere Reserve and is a proposed national park (IUCN/UNEP 1987).

No threatened bird species is known certainly to occur within the area of the proposed park, but it is very likely that the Grey-necked Picathartes *Picathartes oreas* (R) and Bates's Weaver *Ploceus batesi* (R) do so, and the Dja River Warbler *Bradypterus grandis* (K) may also do so (although it is not a forest-dependent species). The primate fauna of the area is rich and mammals present include Gorilla *Gorilla gorilla* (V), Chimpanzee *Pan troglodytes* (V), Elephant *Loxodonta africana* (V) and Leopard *Panthera pardus* (V) (Oates 1986, IUCN/UNEP 1987).

The forest is not threatened, being "almost completely surrounded by the Dja River and thus ... a natural unit"; the process of establishment as a national park was expected to take six years from 1982 (Gartlan 1982b). A preliminary management plan for a national park has been drafted, but no progress has yet been made to implement it (A. P. M. van der Zon *in litt.* 1987). An inventory of the mammals and birds of the forest will soon be carried out (A. P. M. van der Zon *in litt.* 1987).

17. Forests in Gabon
The Grey-necked Picathartes *Picathartes oreas* (R) and the Gabon Batis *Batis minima* (n-t) (the latter endemic to Gabon) are sympatric in many places in north-east Gabon (Brosset and Erard 1986), but data on exact localities are lacking and no detailed attempt is therefore made here to identify important sites. Nicoll and Langrand (1986a) and Oates (1986) have recommended the establishment of a reserve in north-eastern Gabon; there is a centre of plant diversity, with an exceptional number of endemic species, astride the Gabon–Cameroon border (R. Madams *in litt.* 1987), which such a reserve should

presumably help protect. In addition to the birds, this would also be important for Gorillas *Gorilla gorilla* (V), Mandrills *Papio sphinx* (V) and Crested Mangabeys *Cercocebus galeritus* (Oates 1986). The Lopé Reserve, covering some 5,000 sq km in central Gabon, is a locality for the Grey-necked Picathartes, and quite likely for the Gabon Batis as well (Nicoll and Langrand 1986a, C. E. G. Tutin *in litt.* 1987). Primates include the Gorilla, Mandrill, Black Colobus *Colobus satanus* (E) and Golden Potto *Arctocebus calabarensis* (Nicoll and Langrand 1986a, Oates 1986). To the east of the Lopé Reserve in the Forêt des Abeilles a new species of primate was recently discovered, the Sun-tailed Monkey *Cercopithecus* sp. (Oates 1986). This area is also likely to be important for birds. Nicoll and Langrand (1986a) make recommendations for the improved management of existing reserves in Gabon and this now requires follow-up. More detailed biological surveys of these forests are also needed.

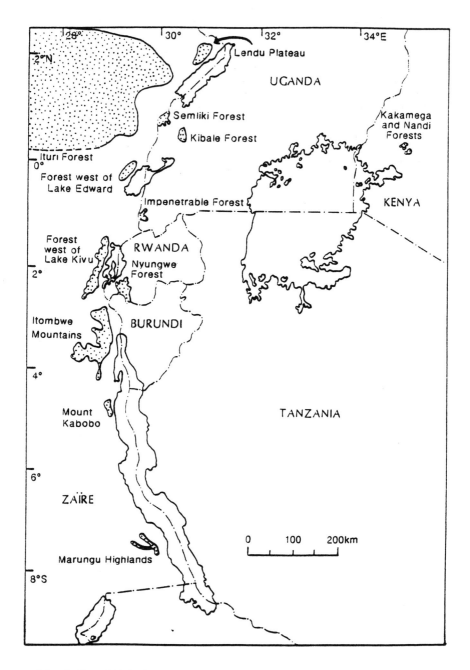

Map 4: Central Refugium

CENTRAL REFUGIUM

The forests of the Central Refugium are those in eastern Zaïre, south-western Uganda, Rwanda and Burundi which flank the Albertine Rift Valley. Both lowland and montane forests are included in this section. A few outlying forests with similar avifaunas, such as Kakamega Forest in western Kenya, are also treated here as belonging to this group. Previous accounts of the forest bird conservation problems have been given by Dowsett (1985) and Prigogine (1985). In this review we identify 12 forests of particular importance for forest bird conservation in the region:

No.	Forest area	Priority score	Position among all the forests in this review
27	Itombwe Mountains, Zaïre	40	5
19	Ituri Forest, Zaïre	31	7
26	Forest west of Lake Kivu, Zaïre	14	27
25	Nyungwe Forest, Rwanda	13	28=
23	Forest west of Lake Edward, Zaïre	12	32=
18	Lendu Plateau, Zaïre	10	37=
29	Marungu Highlands, Zaïre	10	37=
24	Impenetrable Forest, Uganda	9	44=
21	Kibale Forest, Uganda	8	50=
28	Mount Kabobo, Zaïre	8	50=
22	Kakamega and Nandi Forests, Kenya	6	56=
20	Semliki Forest, Uganda	6	56=

Details of the priority scores and how they are calculated are given in the introductory section "Priorities for Conservation Action". It will be noted that the Itombwe Mountains and Ituri Forest are of particular importance, these ranking first and third respectively among the forests on the African mainland. Map 4 shows the geographic locations of these 12 key conservation areas.

The avifauna of the Albertine Rift forests still requires a great deal more survey work (P. C. Howard *in litt.* 1987), especially in Zaïre (J. Verschuren *in litt.* 1986). Some interesting forest bird communities which did not qualify for inclusion in this review occur on the Virunga Volcanoes (Zaïre, Uganda and Rwanda), Idjwi Island (Zaïre) and Mahale Mountain (western Tanzania). Nevertheless, the extreme importance of both the Itombwe Mountains and the Ituri Forest is beyond doubt.

18. Lendu Plateau (Zaïre)   2°05'N 30°50'E
This is a large area of high ground on the west side of Lake Albert in north-east Zaïre, bordered in the north by the Ugandan frontier. There is no official protection for whatever forest remains.

Prigogine's Greenbul *Chlorocichla prigoginei* (V) and Chapin's Flycatcher

N. J. Collar and S. N. Stuart

Muscicapa lendu (R) occur on the Lendu Plateau, as do the near-threatened White-naped Pigeon *Columba albinucha*, Chapin's Flycatcher-babbler *Lioptilus chapini* and Bedford's Paradise Flycatcher *Terpsiphone bedfordi*.

The status of forests in the area is wholly unknown and a survey is urgently needed to determine what conservation measures are needed there (Prigogine 1985).

19. Ituri Forest (Zaïre)   1°00'N 29°00'E

The Ituri Forest is a huge area of 60,000 to 70,000 sq km in north-eastern Zaïre, south of the Uele District. The southern edge is at approximately 0° latitude, the northern and eastern edges are defined by the forest-savanna ecotone and the Semliki River (in the east), and the western edge is at about 27° or 28°E. The southernmost part of the Ituri Forest is conserved in the northern part of Maiko National Park (J. Verschuren *in litt.* 1986) . The western and eastern areas of the forest are somewhat distinct from each other biologically (J. Hart *in litt.* 1987). The western area is centred around the Epulu and Ituri Rivers, and the eastern area is centred south of Irumu and extends south to the border of the Virunga National Park (including Mount Hoyo) and east to the Ugandan border. A small part of the easternmost extension of the forest is conserved in the Virunga National Park in the Semliki Valley (J. Verschuren *in litt.* 1986). The altitude ranges from 700 to 1,500 m and the climate is humid with about 2,000 mm of rain per annum (J. Hart *in litt.* 1987). The vegetation is tall, closed, evergreen lowland rainforest with some savanna patches and forest-savanna mosaic at the margins. The dominant trees are *Cynometra alexandri*, *Brachystegia laerrentia* and *Gilbertiodendron dewevrei* (J. Hart *in litt.* 1987). The *Gilbertiodendron* forests are species-poor, but the other forest-types are noted for their richness (J. Hart *in litt.* 1987). Ituri is one of the largest intact forests remaining on the rim of the Zaïre basin; it is important as the home of the Mbuti pygmies. Human population density is 0.5 to 2.0 per sq km, mostly concentrated along the few roads. Most of the forest has no permanent settlements (J. Hart *in litt.* 1987).

Nahan's Francolin *Francolinus nahani* (R), the Forest Ground-thrush *Turdus oberlaenderi* (R), Golden-naped Weaver *Ploceus aureonucha* (I) and Yellow-legged Weaver *P. flavipes* (V) all occur in the eastern part of the Ituri Forest, Turner's Eremomela *Eremomela turneri* (R) has recently been recorded there, and Prigogine's Greenbul *Chlorocichla prigoginei* (V) is known from the extreme south-east of the forest. The two weavers are endemic to Ituri Forest. The near-threatened White-naped Pigeon *Columba albinucha* and Sassi's Olive Greenbul *Phyllastrephus lorenzi* occur in Ituri. The Congo Peacock *Afropavo congensis* (n-t) may occur in the extreme southern Ituri Forest (the first record – the 1913 feather – was from the type-locality of the Yellow-legged Weaver). The eastern area of the Ituri Forest is especially rich in bird species, and of those listed above, the pigeon and the two greenbuls are unknown in the better conserved western area (J. Hart *in litt.* 1987). The Ituri Forest is the most important locality for the Okapi *Okapia johnstoni*, and numerous other forest animals, such as the rare Aquatic Civet *Osbornictis piscivora*, occur there (Sidle and Lawson 1986, J. Hart *in litt.* 1987); rare primates include the Owl-faced Guenon *Cercopithecus hamlyni* (K) and L'hoest's Monkey *C. lhoesti* (V) (Oates 1986), and in all 13 primate species occur in Ituri, "the richest assemblage recorded from any forest in Africa" (Hart *et al.* 1986).

Plans are afoot to establish a large protected area, possibly a national park, in the western area of the Ituri Forest (Sidle and Lawson 1986), which would serve as an essential means of conserving the two weavers and the Okapi. Preliminary actions to establish such a reserve or park have been outlined (Sidle and Lawson 1986). However, the rich and important eastern area remains at serious risk of deforestation (J. Hart *in litt.* 1987). Some sort of protected area needs to be established in the eastern Ituri, especially around Mount Hoyo, as a north-western extension of the Virunga National Park (Prigogine 1985). Adequate protection of Ituri is important because it ranks 7th among the forests considered in this review (3rd for the African mainland) with a very high score of 31.

20. Semliki (Bwamba) Forest (Uganda)   0°45'N 30°05'E

Semliki Forest lies on the east bank of the Semliki River in Bwamba County, westernmost Uganda, north of the Rwenzori range. It covers roughly 220 sq km of undulating terrain, ranging from 650 to 1,000 m, intersected by deep broad valleys carrying water to the Semliki River, and stands on poorly drained, saline clay soils that have low agricultural productivity (van Orsdol 1983a). The forests of these valleys, dominated by *Cynometra* (van Orsdol 1983a) and described as dense, high-canopy (c.25 m), rich, wet and evergreen, with a thick, luxuriant undergrowth (Friedmann and Williams 1971) but marked as medium altitude and semi-deciduous (in Downer and Redman 1967), are extensions of the Ituri Forest across the Semliki in Zaïre (q.v.) and form the eastern limit of the Lower Guinea forest block. The temperature is high, humidity near saturation point, and mean annual rainfall around 1,500 mm (Friedmann and Williams 1971, van Orsdol 1983, Howard 1986a). Most of the high-canopy mixed forest characteristic of the better soils in the river valleys has now been destroyed, but some valuable swamp forest remains, as well as large tracts of *Cynometra*-dominated forest (P. C. Howard *in litt.* 1987). The area is a forest reserve and the eastern third of it an animal sanctuary; this latter remains relatively intact, and difficult of access (Howard 1986a).

The Forest Ground-thrush *Turdus oberlaenderi* (R), and the near-threatened White-naped Pigeon *Columba albinucha*, Chestnut Barred Owlet *Glaucidium (capense) castaneum* and Sassi's Olive Greenbul *Phyllastrephus lorenzi* occur in Semliki Forest, the owl being almost endemic to the area. A suggestion in Collar and Stuart (1985) that the thrush might now be extinct in Semliki Forest was based on reports of large-scale habitat destruction; however, a considerable area of forest is known still to survive (Howard 1986a). Almost 400 species of bird, though this includes non-forest species, have been recorded, and 10 mammals present occur nowhere else in East Africa (Howard 1986a).

Despite its being a forest reserve, destruction of Semliki has been severe: it was noted as such in the 1960s (Friedmann and Williams 1971) and the situation now is much worse (van Orsdol 1983a, Howard 1986a,b,c). The reserve suffered serious encroachment during the 1970s when a large part of the western two-thirds was occupied by resident cultivators. Most of these people were evicted in 1983 and returned to their homes in Zaïre. However, people were allowed to return in 1985 to grow "temporary crops", and a survey in April 1986 showed that 290 families then resided in the forest, and another 100-200 were using the reserve to cultivate crops (Howard 1986b). Their eviction would result in little serious hardship and it is also in Uganda's best long-term interests that Semliki remains under management (Howard 1986b). To meet these challenges, a Bwamba Natural Resources Development Project has recently started, attempting to resolve the forestry, agriculture, wildlife and social conflicts in the area, and eviction from the reserve should be complete by April 1987 (Howard 1986c, *in litt.* 1987).

21. **Kibale Forest (Uganda)**   0°30'N 30°30'E
Kibale is situated near the equator in western Uganda. The topography is gently
undulating with forest in some low-iying areas being replaced by swamps and on
hilltops by grassland, the altitude ranging from 1,100 to 1,600 m, with two major
rivers, the Mpanga and Dura, flowing southwards; about 90 percent of the forest
stands on red ferralitic soils (Struhsaker and Leland 1979, van Orsdol 1983b). The
forest is medium-altitude moist evergreen in type, possessing typical features of
lowland tropical rainforest (trees up to 45 m in height, rich in epiphytes) but
distinguished by its higher altitude and lower temperature and rainfall, mean
annual rainfall being c.1,700 mm, with two distinct annual wet seasons, March to
May and September to November (Struhsaker and Leland 1979, Skorupa and
Kasenene 1984; also Malpas 1980, van Orsdol 1983b). In general, the northern
part consists of *Newtonia*, mixed *Chrysophyllum/Celtis durandi* and mixed
Parinari/Strombosia forests, the southern part is dominated by *Pterygota*,
Piptadeniastrum and mixed *Lovoa/Diospyros/Markhamia* forests, and *Cynometra*
forms the dominant community along the Dura River in the south (van Orsdol
1983b). Kibale is a forest reserve, the boundaries of which embrace 560 sq km;
however, in 1987 only 265 sq km of this remained intact, and 60 sq km of this
are protected as a nature reserve (T. T. Struhsaker *in litt.* 1987); there is also a
2 sq km nature reserve and a 12 sq km research plot (van Orsdol 1986). Another
95 sq km is selectively logged or planted with exotic softwoods, but not
encroached upon by agriculturists (T. T. Struhsaker *in litt.* 1987).
    The Kibale Ground-thrush *Turdus kibalensis* (I) is known only from Kibale
Forest. "With eleven species of primate, Kibale is one of the two richest forests
for primates in East Africa and among the very richest in the world" and hosts "a
profusion of other mammals", including African Golden Cat *Felis auratus*
(Struhsaker and Leland 1979). More than 300 species of bird have been recorded
from the Kibale area (T. T. Struhsaker *in litt.* 1987).
    Kibale has suffered serious disturbance (selective logging) in its northern third
and agricultural encroachment in its southern third, and faces the omnipresent
threats of timber theft and further encroachment, as well as poaching (Malpas
1980, van Orsdol 1986). The expansion of the nature reserve to encompass the
remaining intact 265 sq km is very desirable.

22. **Kakamega and Nandi Forests (Kenya)**   0°17'N 34°53'E
These lie adjacent to each other in western Kenya between the towns of
Kakamega and Kapsabet, north-east of Lake Victoria. There are three main forest
blocks, all once connected, namely Kakamega, North Nandi and South Nandi:
Kakamega is flat, at 1,700 m, North and South Nandi lie on a west-facing scarp
and rise to 2,130 m (Diamond 1979, Diamond and Fayad 1979, Mann 1985).
Kakamega and South Nandi are characterised as intermediate evergreen forest with
canopy 25-30 m high, emergent trees up to 45 m, understorey 10-20 m high, plus
a shrub layer and relatively sparse ground cover; they are floristically mixed, with
nothing apparently dominant, though in one area *Olea welwitchii*, *Funtumia
latifolia*, *Manilkara butugi*, *Bosquiea phoberos*, *Teclea nobilis*, *Diospyros
abyssinica*, *Monodora myristica*, *Ficus*, *Celtis africana*, *C. mildbraedii*, *Fagara
macrophylla*, *F. mildbraedii*, *Antiaris toxicaria*, *Cordia abyssinica*, *C. milleni*,
Albizia gummifera (many of these names are now changed – F. Dowsett-Lemaire
in litt. 1987) were important (Zimmerman 1972). Mean annual rainfall in
Kakamega is above 2,000 mm, mean annual temperature around 21°C
(Zimmerman 1972), mean maximum 27.4°C, mean minimum 12.1°C (P. B.

Taylor and C. A. Taylor *in litt.* 1987); the region generally has a rainy season
from April to August, but rain falls in all months, lowest rainfall being from
December to February (Brown and Britton 1980, P. B. Taylor and C. A. Taylor
in litt. 1987). In the late 1960s Kakamega and South Nandi were estimated to
hold less than 480 sq km (120,000 acres), of which half was considered intact
(Zimmerman 1972), but by 1975 only some 350 sq km were thought to remain
(Mann 1985) and in 1979 remote sensing showed that these two held 300 sq km
of forest while North Nandi held 91 sq km (Doute *et al.* 1981); by 1986
Kakamega was judged to be less than 75 percent of its 1979 estimated area (P. B.
Taylor and C. A. Taylor *in litt.* 1987). The whole area of the three forests is
forest reserve (Doute *et al.* 1981), part of Kakamega (11.6 sq km) is a nature
reserve, and 34 sq km of North Nandi is a nature reserve (Cunningham-van
Someren 1982); part of Kakamega is proposed for national park status, but this is
not yet bestowed (*contra* Collar and Stuart 1985).

Turner's Eremomela *Eremomela turneri* (R) and Chapin's Flycatcher *Muscicapa
lendu* (R) are recorded from Kakamega, the former being recorded also from
South Nandi, the latter from North Nandi. The Pygmy Honeyguide *Indicator
pumilio* (n-t) has also been recorded from Kakamega, though the identity of these
specimens is now known to be invalid (Prigogine 1978, L. L. Short and J. F. M.
Horne verbally 1987). A race of Ansorge's Greenbul *Andropadus ansorgei
kavirondensis* is now only known from Kakamega (C. F. Mann *in litt.* 1987). The
first Kenyan record of Dark Mongoose *Crossarchus obscurus* was obtained in
Kakamega in April 1986 (P. B. Taylor and C. A. Taylor *in litt.* 1987). Kakamega
and (to a lesser extent) both Nandi forests contain many species of both plants
and animals that are West or Central African in distribution and occur in Kenya
only in these forests; of the species studied to date, 10-20 percent are of this
type, and the forests are considered internationally important as a continuum
between the distinct biogeographical regions of the Congo Forest and the East
African Highland Forest (Diamond 1979).

Forest in Kakamega is suffering destruction from clearance, selective logging,
cattle-grazing, removal of trees for poles and saplings for fencing and nursery
shade, firewood-gathering, charcoal burning, honey-gathering (by tree-felling) and
complete ring-barking for medicinal purposes (Diamond 1979, Cords 1982, Rowell
1982, H. Oelke *in litt.* 1987); poaching of mammals is widespread (Cords 1982,
P. B. Taylor and C. A. Taylor *in litt.* 1987, H. Oelke *in litt.* 1987). Parts of North
Nandi appear to be threatened by the establishment of plantations for pulp
(Cunningham-van Someren 1982). This precarious conservation situation is the
result of a very high (and ever-increasing) local human population density,
hostility and ignorance of local people in regard to forest protection, high
unemployment, and shortages of guards, patrol vehicles and forest protection funds
(P. B. Taylor and C. A. Taylor *in litt.* 1987). Establishment of a properly
regulated national park in Kakamega is the most obvious step and has been much
discussed; a park has been suggested for an unstudied area of the forest away
from the existing nature reserve, but its formal establishment has yet to take place
(L. L. Short verbally 1987). Apart from this, enforcement of existing regulations
that prohibit exploitation of the Kakamega Forest Reserve is needed (which means
employment of more forest guards) (Cords 1982). Buffer-zones of *Eucalyptus* are
recommended, and (if the national park is not created) the boundaries of the
existing nature reserve should be extended 500 m to the south to include all the
forest between the reserve and the forest station (Cords 1982), an area offering
major opportunities for primate and bird study (P. B. Taylor and C. A. Taylor *in*

litt. 1987). Blocks of forest, e.g. Malaba, not part of the main Kakamega area, also need conservation under any new initiatives (P. B. Taylor and C. A. Taylor *in litt.* 1987). A call has been made for incorporation of conservation into Kenya's Forest Department policy (Diamond 1979); what is needed in Kakamega is a policy to integrate the social and economic needs of the local people with effective conservation of the forest they are currently destroying (H. Oelke *in litt.* 1987).

23. Forest west of Lake Edward (Zaïre)   0°15'S 29°15'E

This area is a large agglomeration of mountains with forest, the only part of which that is currently protected being the region of Mount Tshiaberimu (Tshabirimu) in the north, close to Lake Edward, which is included in the northern section of the Virunga National Park (Prigogine 1985).

The Albertine Owlet *Glaucidium albertinum* (R), Prigogine's Greenbul *Chlorocichla prigoginei* (V) and Grauer's Swamp Warbler *Bradypterus graueri* (V) (not a true forest species) occur in forest west of Lake Edward, as do the near-threatened Congo Peacock *Afropavo congensis*, White-naped Pigeon *Columba albinucha*, Pygmy Honeyguide *Indicator pumilio*, Sassi's Olive Greenbul *Phyllastrephus lorenzi* and Chapin's Flycatcher-babbler *Lioptilus chapini*.

Forest around Alimbongo has been destroyed but large areas of forest in the Lutunguru area (including transition forest on Mount Biakiri) have been recommended for protection through the creation of a reserve east of the Maiko National Park (Prigogine 1985). The high altitude forest on Mount Tshiaberimu (mainly bamboo) is theoretically safeguarded in the Virunga National Park, although there is extensive human encroachment there (J. Verschuren *in litt.* 1986, W. von Richter *in litt.* 1987), but the mid-elevation forests are disappearing rapidly (J. Hart *in litt.* 1987). A survey to determine the extent of the remaining forest and priorities for its protection is urgently needed (J. Hart *in litt.* 1987).

24. Impenetrable (Bwindi) Forest (Uganda)   1°00'S 29°40'E

Impenetrable Forest lies in extreme south-west Uganda, against the frontier with Zaïre. It grows on very hilly and steep terrain ranging from 1,060 m to 2,600 m; mean annual rainfall is about 1,440 mm (Malpas 1980, Butynski 1984, 1985). It covers 321 sq km (Butynski 1985), and has the status of a forest reserve and animal sanctuary (Malpas 1980, Kalina and Butynski 1986); these are two small natural reserves of 4.5 sq km (north) and 8 sq km (south) (Harcourt 1981, Clarke 1987).

The African Green Broadbill *Pseudocalyptomena graueri* (R), Grauer's Swamp Warbler *Bradypterus graueri* (V) and Chapin's Flycatcher *Muscicapa lendu* (R) occur in Impenetrable Forest, although the first of these appears at best very rare and the second is not a forest-dwelling species (see especially Bennun 1986, 1987). The near-threatened Pygmy Honeyguide *Indicator pumilio*, Kivu Ground-thrush *Turdus tanganjicae* and Shelley's Crimson-wing *Cryptospiza shelleyi* also occur there. Over 300 species of bird have now been recorded (T. M. Butynski *in litt.* 1987). The forest also holds a third of the world's Mountain Gorillas *Gorilla gorilla beringei* (E) (Malpas 1980). Nine other species of primate occur, including the Chimpanzee *Pan troglodytes* (V) and L'hoest's Monkey *Cercopithecus lhoesti* (V); Elephant *Loxodonta africana* (V) and possibly still Leopard *Panthera pardus* (V) also occur (Butynski 1984). As one of the few large expanses of forest in East Africa where unbroken vegetation stretches from the lowlands to the mountains, it possesses one of the region's richest faunas and floras (Malpas 1980, Kalina and Butynski 1986).

Use of Impenetrable by local people is permitted in all but 2.5 percent of its total area, and logging is fairly intense in the forestry-designated areas ("coupes"), which cover 18.5 percent of the total area; nevertheless both Impenetrable and its surrounding forest remnants are being overexploited at present (Malpas 1980, Harcourt 1981). Some of the more serious problems are (a) illegal gold prospecting and mining, (b) illegal removal of wood (in 1982-1983 80 percent of timber trees cut were felled illegally), (c) poaching, which is common and widespread and has reduced many large animals to extinction or near-extinction, (d) disturbance from the 500-1,000 people who enter each day to use the forest, in 90 percent of cases in illegal ways and always without the guidance of scientifically sound management policy (Butynski 1984). A permanent field station is needed, five forest remnants outside Impenetrable should be gazetted into the reserve and the whole should be elevated to the status of nature reserve (allowing local usage of only the existing "coupes") or preferably of national park (Malpas 1980, Harcourt 1981, Butynski 1984, 1985, 1986, Bennun 1987).

25. Nyungwe (Rugege) Forest (Rwanda)   2°30'S 29°20'E

This large forest lies in south-west Rwanda against (and athwart) the frontier with Burundi, and immediately south-east of Lake Kivu. Its altitudinal range is from 1,650 to 2,950 m, with a small isolated block between 1,550 and 1,600 m; several different forest-types occur, including large *Podocarpus* forests, bamboo thickets and extensive marsh complexes (Prigogine 1985; also Weber and Vedder 1984). Several different successional stages of forest are present, dominated by species such as *Hagenia*, *Macaranga neomildbreadiana*, *Neoboutonia* and *Musanga*; this is perhaps the result of ancient human disturbance of the habitat (J.-P. Vande weghe *in litt.* 1987). Nyungwe's surface area (in Rwanda) in 1979 was 970 sq km (Monfort 1983, Prigogine 1985), although it is contiguous with the much smaller Kibira Forest in Burundi, since 1982 a national park (Weber and Vedder 1984); the combined area of the two forests is roughly 1,140 sq km (Weber 1987). Nyungwe is currently a forest reserve (Weber and Vedder 1984).

The Albertine Owlet *Glaucidium albertinum* (R), Grauer's Swamp Warbler *Bradypterus graueri* (V) (not a true forest species but restricted to about 1,000 ha of swamp), Kungwe Apalis *Apalis argentea* (R) (restricted to a small area of dry forest), Chapin's Flycatcher *Muscicapa lendu* (R), plus the near-threatened Pygmy Honeyguide *Indicator pumilio*, Kivu Ground-thrush *Turdus tanganjicae*, Red-collared Flycatcher-babbler *Lioptilus rufocinctus* and Shelley's Crimson-wing *Cryptospiza shelleyi*, occur in Nyungwe Forest (which harbours over 200 forest bird species, of which 23 are endemic to the Central Refugium area: Weber and Vedder 1984, J.-P. Vande weghe *in litt.* 1987). Eleven primates also occur, including Chimpanzee *Pan troglodytes* (V) and L'hoest's Monkey *Cercopithecus lhoesti* (V); the fauna and flora are "extremely rich", with "many endemic species" including an endemic race of Weyn's Duiker *Cephalophus weynsi lestradei* (Monfort 1983, Weber and Vedder 1984, Weber 1987). Over 50 species of woody plant are thought to be endemic (J.-P. Vande weghe *in litt.* 1987). In Nyungwe's western sector, lower montane vegetation remains intact down to 1,650 m with over 100 tree species forming a broccoli-headed canopy over a sparse ground-cover (Weber and Vedder 1984).

Clearance along the whole boundary of the forest has reduced it to its present size from 1,140 sq km in 1958; it represents a huge reserve for the production of firewood, charcoal and timber, and cutting along watercourses is widespread

owing to intensive gold-working (Weber and Vedder 1984, Prigogine 1985). A
master management plan is being prepared by the Rwandan government (Weber
and Vedder 1984), and all the best conserved and species-rich areas have been
proposed for total protection as a national park to cover an area of 232 sq km,
with the possibility of a further 167 sq km to be added (Monfort 1983). The
lowest altitude forest zone (1,550-2,000 m), "which must be preserved" (Prigogine
1985), appears to be included in the management proposals, which also allow for
controlled exploitation and reafforestation of 5-10 percent of degraded forest
fringe and a 15-year interdisciplinary study on multiple-use potential for the
remaining forest (Weber and Vedder 1984). The latest version of the management
proposals, yet to be fully accepted by the Rwandan government, recommends an
"integral forest reserve" of 420 sq km (J.-P. Vande weghe in *litt.* 1987). The dry
forest in which the Kungwe Apalis occurs covers only a very small area and is
severely threatened by fires (J.-P. Vande weghe *in litt.* 1987). Gold-mining
activities need curbing and a major Swiss buffer-zone programme for the entire
reserve is to be joined by other donor organisations (Weber and Vedder 1984).
Recent evidence suggests that threats such as gold mining, road building and
illegal selective logging are not currently serious problems in Nyungwe (J.-P.
Vande weghe *in litt.* 1987).

26. Forest west of Lake Kivu (Zaïre)   2°05'S 28°45'E

The mountains that hold this forest extend as a narrow north–south chain along
the entire west shore of Lake Kivu in eastern Zaïre. The Kahuzi-Biega National
Park, which is mapped quite differently in Verschuren (1975) and Prigogine
(1985), presumably owing to the extension of the park in 1975 (W. von Richter
in litt. 1987), is in fact composed of two parts: 600 sq km protects the montane
vegetation west of Lake Kivu up to 3,000 m, while a large western extension
preserves transition and lowland forest; the two parts together comprise about
7,000 sq km (J. Verschuren *in litt.* 1986, W. von Richter *in litt.* 1987).

The African Green Broadbill *Pseudocalyptomena graueri* (R), Grauer's Swamp
Warbler *Bradypterus graueri* (V) and Rockefeller's Sunbird *Nectarinia rockefelleri*
(R) are known from the forested mountains west of Lake Kivu, although the
second of these is not a forest-dwelling species. The near-threatened Congo
Peacock *Afropavo congensis*, White-naped Pigeon *Columba albinucha*, Pygmy
Honeyguide *Indicator pumilio*, Sassi's Olive Greenbul *Phyllastrephus lorenzi*, Kivu
Ground-thrush *Turdus tanganjicae*, Chapin's Flycatcher-babbler *Lioptilus chapini*,
Bedford's Paradise Flycatcher *Terpsiphone bedfordi* and Shelley's Crimson-wing
Cryptospiza shelleyi also occur there. These mountains are also important for
Gorillas *Gorilla gorilla* (V) (Oates 1986, J. Verschuren *in litt.* 1986).

Forest in the Kivu region is generally under great pressure from agriculture and
firewood-gathering by an ever-increasing human population (Mankoto ma
Mbaelele 1984). However, the management of the montane part of Kahuzi-Biega
National Park is known to be reasonably effective (J. Verschuren *in litt.* 1986),
although in the area near Bukavu, and up to 50 km to the north, the forest is
being rapidly cleared by agriculturists (W. von Richter *in litt.* 1987). A survey is
needed to determine whether and by how much the threatened forest-dependent
birds of the area west of Lake Kivu are secured by the Kahuzi-Biega National
Park.

27. Itombwe Mountains (Zaïre)   3°30'S 28°55'E
The Itombwe Mountains run north–south along the Albertine Rift on the west side
of the northernmost stretch of Lake Tanganyika in eastern Zaïre. Several peaks
rise above 3,000 m, the highest being Mt Mohi at 3,475 m; topography is varied
and there are consequently considerable variations in rainfall, humidity and
temperature, with no real dry season (June and July least wet) below 2,000 m,
and with high, even rainfall (with lower temperatures, however, and with a dry
season towards the south) above 2,000 m (Stubbs 1988). Montane forest (forest
above 1,500 m) covers about 10,000 sq km (Prigogine 1980) or, taking
1,600-2,400 m as the extremes, 6,500 sq km, including 1,500 sq km of bamboo
and 500 sq km of gallery forest (Prigogine 1985). On the east side of the range
montane forest is only patchy or in galleries below 2,300 m, while on the west
there is, in descending order, bamboo, montane forest, a grassland zone, then
further montane forest that integrades with lowland forest between 1,200 and
1,800 m; in the montane forest, where the canopy reaches around 25 m, dominant
species of tree are *Parinari* sp., *Carapa* sp., *Homalium* sp., *Syzygium* sp., *Fagara*
aff. *inaequalis*, *Sapium ellipticum*, *Ocotea michelsonii* and *Croton megalocarpus*,
but above 2,000 m the dominants include *Hirtella* sp., *Symphonia* sp., *Olea
hochstetteri*, *Chrysophyllum* sp., and *Ficalhoa laurifolia* (Stubbs 1988). None of
the area is protected.

The Itombwe Owl *Phodilus prigoginei* (I) and Schouteden's Swift
Schoutedenapus schoutedeni (I) are known with certainty only from the Itombwe
Mountains, although their strict dependence on forest is not proven; and the
Albertine Owlet *Glaucidium albertinum* (R), African Green Broadbill
Pseudocalyptomena graueri (R), Forest Ground-thrush *Turdus oberlaenderi* (R),
Chapin's Flycatcher *Muscicapa lendu* (R) and Rockefeller's Sunbird *Nectarinia
rockefelleri* (R) also occur (in forest) there. The near-threatened Congo Peacock
Afropavo congensis, White-naped Pigeon *Columba albinucha*, Pygmy Honeyguide
Indicator pumilio, Sassi's Olive Greenbul *Phyllastrephus lorenzi*, Chapin's
Flycatcher-babbler *Lioptilus chapini*, Red-collared Flycatcher-babbler *L.
rufocinctus*, Kivu Ground-thrush *Turdus tanganjicae*, Bedford's Paradise Flycatcher
Terpsiphone bedfordi and Shelley's Crimson-wing *Cryptospiza shelleyi* are also
present. Of 36 species identified as endemic to the Albertine Rift forests, no
fewer than 32 occur in the Itombwe Mountains (Prigogine 1985). An important
population of Gorillas *Gorilla gorilla* (V) occurs there (Prigogine 1985), Leopards
Panthera pardus (V) are common, and Elephants *Loxodonta africana* (V) are
present in forest patches; two rare forest shrews are known only from single
specimens in the Itombwe range (Stubbs 1988). Among amphibians, at least 21
taxa are recorded from Itombwe above 1,500 m, most being of limited distribution
and six being endemic (Stubbs 1988).

Although the Itombwe Mountains are difficult of access and possess a very low
human population density, Kamituga (just to the north-west of the montane forest
area) is an important mining centre with a large population; there is some danger
of clearance around villages higher in the mountains and cattle-breeding flourishes
on the high plateaus (Prigogine 1985). The area is under severe pressure from
agriculturists and pastoralists (W. von Richter *in litt.* 1987). All montane forest
and two adjacent patches of lowland forest north and south of the upper Elila
River are proposed as forest conservation areas (see Prigogine 1985). The
Itombwe Mountains have an extremely high score of 40, the highest for
continental Africa, and rank 5th among the forests considered in this review. It is
therefore extremely disturbing that no conservation action is taking place, although

an initiative is now being sought by the Fauna and Flora Preservation Society (Stubbs 1988).

28. Mount Kabobo (Zaïre)   4°50'S 29°00'E

This mountain is a rather isolated peak to the west of the northern half of Lake Tanganyika in eastern Zaïre. There is no official protection for whatever forest remains.

The Kabobo Apalis *Apalis kaboboensis* (R) is confined to forest on Mount Kabobo, and the near-threatened Kivu Ground-thrush *Turdus tanganjicae* and Red-collared Flycatcher-babbler *Lioptilus rufocinctus* also occur there. There is an endemic subspecies of the Western Black-and-white Colobus *Colobus polykomos prigoginei* (A. Prigogine *in litt.* 1986).

The status of forests on Kabobo is unknown, but the whole of the mountain forest surrounding the peak must be protected (Prigogine 1985).

29. Marungu Highlands (Zaïre)   7°25'S 29°45'E

The rather extensive area of the Marungus lies to the west of the southern half of Lake Tanganyika in eastern Zaïre. The area consists of two main land masses separated by the low-lying Mulobozi River, the smaller (northern) section (also called the Malimba Mountains) rising to c.2,100 m, the larger (southern) section reaching c.2,460 m; the soil, derived from granitic or rhyolitic rocks, is generally poor in nutrients (Dowsett and Prigogine 1974). Grassland and scrub are the major habitats but there is dense forest (including *Parinari excelsa*, *Teclea nobilis*, *Polyscias fulva*, *Ficus storthophylla* and *Turraea holstii*) in ravines and, more importantly, a narrow riparian forest (with *Syzygium cordatum*, *Ficalhoa laurifolia* and *Ilex mitis*) along streams; mean annual rainfall approaches 1,200 mm, almost all of which falls in the period from October to April, while the mean annual temperature is 19°C with little monthly variation (Dowsett and Prigogine 1974). The riparian forest must have a very small total area and enjoys no protection whatever.

The Marungu Sunbird *Nectarinia prigoginei* (E) is restricted to this riparian forest. The Marungu Highlands are a centre of endemism for plants, with over 300 endemic species (IUCN 1986).

Riparian forest throughout the Marungus is under severe threat from timber-felling and from the erosion of stream banks by cattle, the result of which will be not only the extinction of the montane bird populations but also the destabilisation of the water supply on which ranching in the Marungus is dependent (Dowsett and Prigogine 1974). Forests bordering the Mulobozi and Lufuko Rivers above 1,500 m are proposed as conservation belts (see Prigogine 1985).

EAST AFRICA

This section includes the belt of montane and lowland forest patches which runs from the Kenyan and Tanzanian coasts in a south-westerly direction through Malawi, western Mozambique and eastern Zimbabwe. Previous accounts of the forest bird conservation problems of this region are given by Lamprey (1975), Dowsett (1985) and Stuart (1985). In this review we identify 21 forests of particular importance for forest bird conservation in the region:

No.	Forest area	Priority score	Position among all the forests in this review
31	Sokoke Forest, Kenya	34	6
34	Usambara Mountains, Tanzania	30	8
39	Uzungwa Mountains, Tanzania	29	9=
38	Uluguru Mountains, Tanzania	20	23=
37	Pugu Hills, Tanzania	12	32=
30	Lower Tana riverine forests, Kenya	10	37=
45	Mount Thyolo, Malawi	10	37=
41	Mount Namuli, Mozambique	10	37=
32	Taita Hills, Kenya	9	44=
33	South-eastern coastal forests, Kenya	9	44=
42	Mount Chiradzulu, Malawi	9	44=
44	Mount Mulanje, Malawi	9	44=
43	Mount Soche, Malawi	9	44=
50	Coastal forests in Sofala, Mozambique	6	56=
46	Mount Chiperone, Mozambique	6	56=
35	Nguru Mountains, Tanzania	5	63=
49	Chirinda Forest, Zimbabwe	5	63=
48	Vumba Highlands, Zimbabwe	5	63=
47	Gorongosa Mountain, Mozambique	4	71=
40	Southern Highlands, Tanzania	4	71=
36	Ukaguru Mountains, Tanzania	4	71=

Details of the priority scores and how they are calculated are given in the introductory section "Priorities for Conservation Action". Many of the forests listed here are particularly small and the conservation problems are therefore very serious. Map 5 shows the geographic locations of these 21 key conservation areas. The forest avifauna of the region is better known than that in the previous three, but there are probably still important areas yet to be discovered, especially in northern and coastal Tanzania and Mozambique. Nevertheless, the Sokoke Forest and the Usambara and Uzungwa Mountains are of undoubted very high priority and rank 2nd, 4th and 5th= respectively among the forests on the African mainland.

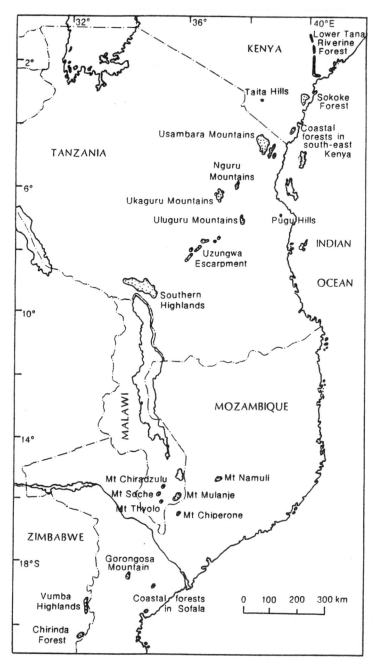

Map 5: East Africa

30. Lower Tana riverine forests (Kenya)   estuary: 2°30'S 40°30'E

The forests of concern here lie in patches along the floodplain of the Tana River from its estuary upstream as far as Bura. The whole area is a very flat, featureless, semi-arid plain, on alluvial soils; the river is highly meandering, with many ox-bow lakes, so that the forest is a mosaic of depressions, levees and point bars (Hughes 1984). The vegetation patterns are accordingly varied with many successional types in close juxtaposition (Andrews *et al.* 1975); a number of forest-types can be identified, including those on the forest edge dominated by *Acacia elatior* or *A. clavigera*, forests on levees with *Ficus sycamorus, Pachystela brevipes, Sorindeia madagascariensis, Trichilia emetica* and *Sterculia appendiculata,* and forests on heavy clays dominated by *Garcinia livingstonei, Diospyros mespiliformis* and *Mimusops fruticosa* (Andrews *et al.* 1975, Marsh 1976, 1986, Hughes 1988). Mean annual rainfall rises from 500 to 1,000 mm towards the coast, falling mainly in May and June, also November and December, temperature being between 22 and 34°C at Hola (Andrews *et al.* 1975; details in Hughes 1984). Forest for the whole length of the Tana covers only 59 sq km, and from the maps providing this information (Doute *et al.* 1981) less than half appears to lie below Bura.   The Tana River National Primate Reserve and the Arawale National Reserve protect an unknown proportion of these forests. Witu (at the estuary) is a "government forest" (Cunningham-van Someren 1982).

East Coast Akalat *Sheppardia gunningi* (R) and Spotted Ground-thrush *Turdus fischeri* (R) (a non-breeding visitor) have been recorded from the lower Tana River (the latter at Kipini by the estuary). The near-threatened Southern Banded Snake Eagle *Circaetus fasciolatus*, White-winged Apalis *Apalis chariessa* (possibly extinct at this locality), Plain-backed Sunbird *Anthreptes reichenowi* and Uluguru Violet-backed Sunbird *A. neglectus* are also recorded from lower Tana forests. Tana forests are of major importance as the only home of the Tana River Red Colobus *Colobus badius rufomitratus* (E) and Tana River Mangabey *Cercocebus galeritus galeritus* (E). However, both these species have decreased dramatically in recent years, the colobus from 1,200-1,800 individuals in 1975 to 200-300 in 1986, and the mangabey from 1,100-1,500 in 1975 to 800-1,100 in 1986 (Marsh 1986, Decker 1987). Hunter's Antelope *Damaliscus hunteri* (R) occurs in the Arawale National Reserve (which was created to protect it) and is occasionally seen in the Primate Reserve (B. S. Decker *in litt.* 1987, East 1988). Tana forests hold a poplar *Populus ilicifolia* that grows on sandy substrates at the river's edge and is endemic to a few East African rivers (Hughes 1987, F. M. R. Hughes verbally 1987).

The damming (four dams completed) and proposed damming (one dam under construction, five more envisaged) of the upper Tana River (Hughes 1987) are likely to cause severe disruption of the flooding regime (and the pattern of sediment deposition) downstream, with probably deleterious consequences for the riverine forests (Marsh 1986). Encroachment and over-exploitation for firewood and charcoal (especially near the Bura irrigation scheme) are considered to be serious (Hughes 1984, 1987). The proposed Tana Delta Rice Project, as mapped in Hughes (1987), appears to threaten the whole Kipini forest. The Primate Reserve requires enlargement and forest conservation needs full integration with the Bura irrigation scheme; further research and improved management of the Primate Reserve are called for by Marsh (1986). A research project is continuing on the two primate species, which is certain to result in additional conservation recommendations.

31. Sokoke Forest   (Kenya)   3°20'S 39°55'E
The Arabuko-Sokoke Forest lies in eastern Kenya near the coast south-west of
Malindi. Topography is flat, coastal plain, the forest lying athwart dark red,
infertile magarini sand-soil, forming a shelf 60 m above sea-level, and a variety
of loose and compact sands and coral rag bordering the coastal belt (Kelsey and
Langton 1984). Six forest-types exist: (1) woodland dominated by *Brachystegia
spiciformis* (on loose sandy soils), with cycads *Encephalartos hildebrandtii* present
in more closed canopy areas; (2) *Cynometra–Manilkara–Brachylaena* forest (on
red soils) in two separate regions in the south-west and north-east, understorey
also with cycads, plus shrubs and lianas; (3) *Cynometra* thicket with *Brachylaena*
trees, covering a large area of the north-west; (4) *Cynometra–Afzelia* forest (on
white soil), a small patch in north-central Sokoke; (5) *Afzelia* rainforest, with a
high species diversity; (6) undifferentiated lowland rainforest with *Afzelia
quanzensis*, *Gardenia*, *Combretum schumannii*, *Majidea zanguebarica* and
Hymenaea verrucosa (Kelsey and Langton 1984). Mean annual rainfall is over
1,000 mm in the wettest parts (Kelsey and Langton 1984); there are no
temperature data. The total area of forest (inside the Forest Reserve) is
372 sq km, which breaks down by forest-type as listed above as 67, 111, 131, 11,
35 and 17 sq km respectively; virtually no forest exists outside the forest reserve
and indeed only 28 percent of existing forest is in primary condition (Kelsey and
Langton 1984).   A nature reserve covering 43 sq km exists within the forest
reserve (Britton and Zimmerman 1979) but is not secure as cutting occurs
regularly within it (Kelsey 1986, L. L. Short and J. F. M. Horne verbally 1987).
    The Sokoke Scops Owl *Otus ireneae* (E) and Clarke's Weaver *Ploceus golandi*
(E) are wholly endemic to Sokoke, and the Sokoke Pipit *Anthus sokokensis* (V),
East Coast Akalat *Sheppardia gunningi* (R), Spotted Ground-thrush *Turdus fischeri*
(R) (a non-breeding visitor) and Amani Sunbird *Anthreptes pallidigaster* (R), plus
the near-threatened Southern Banded Snake Eagle *Circaetus fasciolatus* and the
Plain-backed Sunbird *Anthreptes reichenowi*, also occur there.   Aders's Duiker
Cephalophus adersi (V) is found only in Sokoke and on Zanzibar (Pakenham
1979, East 1988), and has not been seen in the former for several years, despite a
recent attempt to trap specimens (Kelsey 1986). The Golden-rumped
Elephant-shrew *Rhynchocyon chrysopygus* is nearly endemic to Sokoke Forest
(Rathbun 1979), and an important population of the very rare and distinctive
subspecies of the Bushy-tailed Mongoose *Bdeogale crassicauda omnivora*
(probably not a forest animal) also occurs (Taylor 1986, 1987; R. Wirth *in litt.*
1986). There are some interesting and increasingly important populations of
Elephant *Loxodonta africana* (V) and Black Rhinoceros *Diceros bicornis* (E)
(L. L. Short *in litt.* 1987).
    The major threat has been from widespread selective logging, resulting in
disturbance and degradation of forest, with particularly serious effects in *Afzelia*
forest, where even within the nature reserve major chainsaw extraction was
observed in July 1987 (M. G. Kelsey *in litt.* 1987); other areas have been cleared
for plantations (Collar and Stuart 1985). Sokoke is presently included within a
major WWF-sponsored Coastal Forest Survey initiative to survey the flora of all
the remaining coastal forests (S. A. Robertson *in litt.* 1988) and a collaborative
conservation plan is under discussion between the National Museums of Kenya
and ICBP (J. H. Fanshawe *in litt.* 1988). Sokoke Forest has a very high score of
34 and ranks 6th among the forests considered in this review (and 2nd among the
forests on the African mainland).

32. Taita Hills   (Kenya)   3°25'S 38°20'E

These lie in south-eastern Kenya immediately west of Voi. They are a steep, uplifted block rising to 2,228 m; such forest as remains (there are two main patches, Ngaongao and Mbololo) is montane in character, holding *Ocotea usambarensis* and *Podocarpus falcatus* (extensive list in Cunningham-van Someren 1982) and has a dense understorey (Collins and Clifton 1984). Ngaongao is drier in the north than in the south, and this difference is reflected in the south's greater density of lianas and epiphytes; dominant canopy species, reaching 35-40 m, are *Aningeria adolfi-friedericii*, *Albizia gummifera* and *Macaranga conglomerata*, and middle and lower layers of vegetation are absent in the relatively few places where the canopy is closed and disturbance minimal (Tetlow 1987). Mean annual rainfall is 1,270 mm (Collins and Clifton 1984); there are no temperature data. Forest cover has been recorded as just 450 ha for the two main patches (Collins and Clifton 1984), although a figure of 820 ha is cited for the whole range, excluding plantations (Doute *et al.* 1981); however, Ngaongao is reported to cover 92 ha, while Mbololo is 168 ha, with the four other forest patches totalling less than 33 ha (Tetlow 1987, Beentje *et al.* 1987, Beentje and Ndiang'ui in prep.). All such forest is designated national forest (Collins and Clifton 1984).

The Taita Thrush *Turdus helleri* (E), Taita Apalis *Apalis (thoracica) fascigularis* (n-t) and the Taita White-eye *Zosterops (poliogaster) silvanus* (n-t) all occur on the Taita Hills, the latter two being endemic to the site. There is an endemic back-fanged snake *Amblyodipsas teitana* and an endemic caecilian *Afrocaecilia teitana*; three butterflies, the Taita Glider *Cymothoe teita* (V), Taita Charaxes *Charaxes xiphares desmondi* (V) and Taita Blue-banded Papilio *Papilio desmondi teita* (E) are endemic to the Taita Hills, as are 13-14 plant taxa, namely *Impatiens engleri* ssp. *pubescens*, *I. teitensis* ssp. *teitensis*, *Memecylon teitense*, *Zimmermannia ovata* (only in Ngaongao), *Dorstenia* cf sp. nov. (possibly endemic), *Millettia oblata* ssp. *teitensis*, *Diphasiopsis fadenii*, *Chassalia discolor*, *Coffea fadenii*, *Psychotria crassipetala*, *P. petitii*, *P.* sp. B of FTEA (only in Ngaongao), *Saintpaulia teitensis* and *Ypsilopus* sp. nov. (both these last only in Mbololo); 37 other rare plants occur there (Collins and Clifton 1984, Beentje and Ndiang'ui in prep.).

There is an increasing human population in the Taita Hills and the areas of forest that remain must be at ever greater risk, especially while they retain only national forest status (Collins and Clifton 1984). Ngaongao is heavily disturbed and logged, with only 50 percent of the area being in primary or lightly disturbed condition (McGuigan 1987). The comprehensive faunal survey of the Taita Hills, recommended in Collar and Stuart (1985), has now been started by the National Museums of Kenya with the participation of Cambridge University (e.g. McGuigan 1987, Tetlow 1987, Beentje and Ndiang'ui in prep.), and the conservation of the area is expected to be addressed in the Danish International Development Agency's Taita-Taveta Development Project (Drapkin 1987). It has been suggested that the forests on the Taita Hills should be set aside as "sites of special scientific interest" (Beentje *et al.* 1987). Investigation of the relatively close mountain Kasigau, where the Taita Thrush has been found (Collar and Stuart 1985), might lead to some range extensions of other endemic Taita forms, and Kasigau itself might then become an object of conservation concern.

33. Coastal forests of south-east Kenya   Shimba Hills: 4°15'S 39°25'E

These comprise Shimba Hills, forests on small hills (Muhaka, Gongoni, Jombo,

Buda, Mrima, Gonja), and forests on coral rag (Jadini [=Diani] and Shimoni), all lying between Mombasa and the Tanzanian border. The Shimba Hills are a steeply rising dissected plateau, attaining 448 m at Pengo Hill, composed of grit and sandstone, and consist of a mosaic of habitat-types (forest, bush, scrub, grassland), the forest dividing into three types: (1) a relic, species- (especially Rubiaceae-) rich forest on deep red soil (probably magarini sand) with *Chlorophora excelsa* (up to 40 m), *Bombax rhodognaphalon*, *Mimusops aedificatoria*, *Pachystela brevipes* and *Combretum schumannii*; (2) forest of *Paramacrolobium coeruleum*, sometimes in association with *Afzelia quanzensis*, *Erythrophleum guineense* and *Brachystegia spiciformis*; and (3) riverine forest, close to *Chlorophora* forest but with many specifically riparian species (Glover 1968). Mean annual rainfall is around 1,240 mm (maximum in July/August, minimum in January/February), but temperature data are incomplete (see Glover 1968, Ross 1981); the area of forest in 1975 was 130 sq km, the majority of it being included in the Shimba Hills National Reserve, which is somewhat larger (see map in Glover 1968; Doute *et al.* 1981, IUCN/UNEP 1987); areas of forest outside the reserve have now been settled (Ross 1981), and National Reserve status means forestry activity may continue (K. Greer *in litt.* 1987). The small hill forests grow on ancient igneous rock; although probably holding distinct floras, the wet forests are structurally similar (Britton *et al.* 1980); Jadini is 0.95 sq km, Shimoni apparently being too small to be mapped (Doute *et al.* 1981), and neither appears to be protected. The even smaller Kaya Forests north of Mombasa are of very high botanical interest (Hawthorne 1985) but remain unknown ornithologically.

East Coast Akalat *Sheppardia gunningi* (R) is recorded from Shimba Hills and Shimoni; Spotted Ground-thrush *Turdus fischeri* (R) (a non-breeding visitor) is recorded from Mrima, Jadini and Shimoni; Plain-backed Sunbird *Anthreptes reichenowi* (n-t) is recorded from Shimba Hills, Mrima and Jadini; Uluguru Violet-backed Sunbird *A. neglectus* (n-t) is recorded from Shimba Hills and Jadini (additional references: Britton 1980, Britton *et al.* 1980). The Southern Banded Snake Eagle *Circaetus fasciolatus* (n-t) is also known from this area. Leopard *Panthera pardus* (V), Elephant *Loxodonta africana* (V) and Kenya's only population of the Sable Antelope *Hippotragus niger* occur in Shimba Hills (Glover 1968, Ross 1981). The restricted Black-and-rufous Elephant-shrew *Rhynchocyon petersi* occurs in these forests, and the distinctive subspecies of the Bushy-tailed Mongoose *Bdeogale crassicauda omnivora* is probably also present (Kingdon 1974a, 1977). Both of Kenya's endemic frog species, *Afrixalus sylvaticus* and *Hyperolius rubrovermiculatus*, are confined to the Shimba Hills and believed to be endangered (Duff-Mackay 1980). The Shimbas also hold an endemic liana *Dichapetalum fructuosum* and an endemic Rubiaceae *Oxyanthus pyriformis* ssp. *brevitubus* (Hawthorne 1985). Buda holds a "severely endangered" endemic liana *Ancistrocladus robertsoniorum* (Hawthorne 1985).

Selective logging of *Chlorophora* forest continues to occur in the Shimba Hills for plantation forest, despite a government decree protecting all indigenous hardwood trees (Ross 1981, K. Greer *in litt.* 1987); other deficiencies are outlined in IUCN/UNEP (1987), and the situation there is regarded as very precarious, with conservation work urgently needed (K. Greer *in litt.* 1987). The Shimba Hills are a major water catchment area for Kenya's south coast (Ross 1981). Some of the small hill forests are difficult of access (Britton *et al.* 1980) and their conservation status is unclear; Mrima, however, was possibly at risk as geological exploration was due to start there in 1981 (Britton *et al.* 1980). There has also been clearance of forests for settlements around Mrima, separating it from the formerly contiguous forests of the lowland plains to the north and east (Britton *et al.* 1980). There appears to be little information on the threats to the forests on coral rag, although Jadini is now largely cleared for coastal hotel complexes (K. Greer *in litt.* 1987, S. M. Wells verbally 1987). All these sites are the target of a major WWF-sponsored initiative to survey the flora of coastal forests by the Herbarium of the National Museums of Kenya (S. A. Robertson *in litt.* 1988). A call has been made for incorporation of conservation into Kenya's Forest Department policy (Diamond 1979).

34. Usambara Mountains (Tanzania)   4°40'S 38°20'E

The Usambaras lie in the Tanga region of north-eastern Tanzania. They divide into two main blocks (East and the much larger West Usambaras), separated by the Lwengera valley, the East Usambaras being a steeply scarped plateau between 900 and 1,050 m rising to a peak (Mount Nilo) at 1,500 m, the West Usambaras also a steeply scarped plateau but much more dissected and rugged, generally between 1,200 and 2,000 m, with a peak (Hambayo) at 2,250 m in the extreme west; there are three small outlying peaks to the east of the East Usambaras (north to south: Mtai, Mhinduro and Mlinga) and one south-west of the West Usambaras (Mafi), all with forest (Stuart 1983). The mountains owe their origin to block-faulting and slow uplift, the rocks are precambrian, crystalline, with a few intrusive igneous bodies, and the soils are laterised red and yellow, derived from acid rocks and of loamy character, free-draining and friable (Stuart 1983). The remaining forest is roughly divisible into three altitudinal levels: lowland evergreen forest (below 800 m), of uneven canopy at 20-30 m, dominated by *Antiaris toxicaria*, *Sterculia appendiculata*, *Trema orientalis*, *Chlorophora excelsa*, *Ficus* and *Albizia*, with numerous lianas and cycads *Encephalartos hildebrandtii* (this forest-type is now mainly in the East Usambara foothills); intermediate evergreen forest (800-1,400 m), one of the most luxuriant types of forest in East Africa, with important species *Macaranga capensis*, *Allanblackia stuhlmannii*, *Myrianthus arboreus*, *Parinari excelsa*, *Cephalosphaera usambarensis* and *Newtonia buchananii* (the last becoming the canopy dominant in the higher parts), and with rich quantities of epiphytes, ferns, mosses and lianas; and highland evergreen forest (1,400 m to summits), dominated by *Ocotea usambarensis*, *Chrysophyllum gorungosanum* and *Podocarpus falcatus*, trees remaining tall at 30 m, occasionally up to 60 m (but generally much lower on the ridges), with ferns and mosses common (Stuart 1983; also Moreau 1935, van der Willigen and Lovett 1981, SNS). On the far west (rainshadow area) of the West Usambaras is a dry "cedar" (= *Juniperus*) forest (Moreau 1935). Rainfall, which is relatively well distributed throughout the year, decreases east to west, from 2,000 mm in East Usambara forests to 1,200 mm in parts of the West Usambaras (excluding *Juniperus*), with peaks from March to May (long rains) and October to December (short rains); possibly owing to proximity to the sea, temperatures are abnormally low for respective altitudes, with frosts not uncommon at 1,800 m between June and August, mean annual temperature at Amani (900 m) 21°C and at Mazumbai (1,500 m) 19.6°C (Stuart 1983). There are approximately 75 sq km, 170 sq km and 210 sq km of lowland, intermediate and highland evergreen forest respectively (calculated from detailed information in Stuart 1983). The majority of these forests are national forest reserves (Stuart 1983).

Seven threatened bird species occur in the Usambaras, two of which, the Usambara Eagle Owl *Bubo vosseleri* (R) and Usambara Ground Robin

Dryocichloides montanus (R) are endemic, the others being Dappled Mountain
Robin *Modulatrix orostruthus* (R), Long-billed Apalis *Apalis moreaui* (R) (known
otherwise from a very small area of northern Mozambique), Amani Sunbird
Anthreptes pallidigaster (R), Banded Green Sunbird *A. rubritorques* (R) and
Tanzanian Mountain Weaver *Ploceus nicolli* (R). The mountain forests also hold
the near-threatened Southern Banded Snake Eagle *Circaetus fasciolatus*,
Plain-backed Sunbird *Anthreptes reichenowi* and Uluguru Violet-backed Sunbird *A.
neglectus*. Swynnerton's Squirrel *Paraxerus vexillarius*, a good species (SNS,
contra speculation in Kingdon 1974b), is wholly restricted to forest in the West
Usambaras and is the only mammal known to be endemic to the range, with the
exception of a new species of shrew *Crocidura tanzaniana* (Hutterer 1986);
Leopards *Panthera pardus* (V) also occur there (SNS). The restricted Black-and-
rufous Elephant-shrew *Rhynchocyon petersi* is common in the Usambaras (SNS)
and there is one specimen record of the distinctive subspecies of the Bushy-tailed
Mongoose *Bdeogale crassicauda omnivora* (R. Wirth *in litt.* 1986). Abbott's
Duiker *Cephalophus spadix* (K) also occurs in the Usambaras (East 1988). Of 22
forest lizards, 15 snakes and 15 anurans, no fewer than 14, two and eight
respectively are endemic (Rodgers and Homewood 1982a). The invertebrate fauna,
though very incompletely studied, has similarly high levels of endemism, hence
(e.g.) two endemic butterflies, up to 27 such wasps, up to 25 such carnivorous
snails, etc. (details in Wells *et al.* 1983). Of at least 276 tree species over 10 m
tall, about 50 are endemic or nearly so, three of them, *Cephalosphaera
usambarensis*, *Englerodendron usambarense* and *Platypterocarpus tanganyikensis*,
being in monotypic genera (further details of floral values in Rodgers and
Homewood 1982a). Nine African violets *Saintpaulia* spp. are endemic to the
Usambaras, five in the East, four in the West (Johansson 1978).
    Rapidly increasing human pressure on the land is the main threat to the forests
of the Usambara Mountains, taking many forms, e.g. timber felling for sawmills,
clearance for subsistence and cash-crop (especially cardamom) cultivation,
firewood-gathering, selection of building poles (Wells *et al.* 1983, SNS). Damage
to highland forest results from *Ocotea* extraction and management to promote
regeneration of *Ocotea* at other trees' expense (Stuart 1983). An indirect source
of threat to remaining forest areas is the highly inaccurate survey by TIRDEP
(Tanga Integrated Rural Development Programme), which has grossly
overestimated the quantity of natural forest remaining: were this to be used as the
basis of conservation or development plans there could be serious consequences
(Stuart 1983). A suite of measures for permanent conservation of the Usambaras
is summarised in Wells *et al.* (1983). IUCN is just starting two major
conservation projects in the East Usambaras, one aimed at managing the timber
production of the forests in a more sustainable way and more effectively
conserving water catchments, and the other concentrating on improving
agricultural output on existing farmland, so reducing the pressure to clear more
forest. Similar projects are now needed in the West Usambaras. Until late 1986
one aid agency was subsidising local sawmills to clear-fell forest in the East
Usambaras. However, this has now been stopped, following objections from
IUCN, aid agencies, and other conservation organisations (see Stuart 1986b). The
Usambara Mountains have a very high score of 30 and rank 8th among the
forests considered in this review.

35. Nguru Mountains (Tanzania)   6°05'S 37°30'E
These lie in the northern part of Morogoro region, eastern Tanzania. They are an

extremely steep, rugged and narrow ridge rising to 2,300 m; on the eastern side rainforest of a type similar to that found in the Usambaras (see below) extends from 400 m up to the peaks, while in the west the forest is much drier (Stuart and van der Willigen 1978, Stuart 1983). Mean annual rainfall appears to be around 1,800 mm (Stuart 1983); no temperature data are known. The estimated area of forest (on both sides of the ridge) is 120 sq km, almost all of it in forest reserves (Stuart 1983).

The Banded Green Sunbird *Anthreptes rubritorques* (R), plus Southern Banded Snake Eagle *Circaetus fasciolatus* (n-t) and Moreau's Sunbird *Nectarinia moreaui* (n-t), occur in the Ngurus (Britton 1980). Two African violets *Saintpaulia* spp. are endemic to the mountains (Johansson 1978).

Forest is generally secure throughout the Ngurus owing to the precipitous nature of the terrain, but there is a danger of clearance in the eastern foothills (SNS). Further survey work is needed to assess the conservation importance of and threats to this area, which is likely to hold other threatened bird species and possibly some endemic animals.

36. Ukaguru Mountains (Tanzania)   6°20'S 36°55'E

These lie south-west of the Nguru Mountains, on the border of Morogoro and Dodoma regions, eastern Tanzania. They are a spectacular uplifted dissected plateau, rising to 2,264 m, but because situated in the rainshadow of the Ulugurus they hold a relatively dry, scrubby montane forest, almost all above 1,500 m; mean annual rainfall is 1,200 mm (Stuart 1983), but there are no temperature data. Forest covers about 100 sq km, almost all of it in forest reserves (SNS).

Mrs Moreau's Warbler *Bathmocercus winifredae* (R) and Moreau's Sunbird *Nectarinia moreaui* (n-t) occur in the Ukagurus.

There is a low human population in the mountains and the only danger at present may (possibly) be from fire (Stuart and van der Willingen 1978). Further survey work is needed to assess the conservation importance of and threats to this area.

37. Pugu Hills (Tanzania)   6°57'S 39°03'E

This is a very small area between (to the north of) Pugu and Kisarawe, in the Dar es Salaam hinterland, eastern Tanzania. The hills are gently sloping and rounded, rising to 305 m, composed of kaolin (china clay); remaining forest is a remnant of East African coastal forests, dominated by *Commiphora zimmermannii*, *Albizia gummifera*, *Cynometra*, *Chlorophora excelsa* (further details in Howell 1981). Mean annual rainfall is 1,236 mm, with a dry season from around June to October (Howell 1981, SNS); there are no temperature data. The area of forest is 10 sq km, although the forest reserve intended to protect it covers 22 sq km (Howell 1981).

Sokoke Pipit *Anthus sokokensis* (V), East Coast Akalat *Sheppardia gunningi* (R) and Spotted Ground-thrush *Turdus fischeri* (R) (a passage migrant in May) occur in the Pugu Hills, as do the near-threatened Southern Banded Snake Eagle *Circaetus fasciolatus* and Uluguru Violet-backed Sunbird *Anthreptes neglectus*. Leopards *Panthera pardus* (V) occur there (Howell 1981), as does the restricted Black-and-rufous Elephant-shrew *Rhynchocyon petersi* (SNS). The almost totally unknown toad *Bufo lyndneri* is recorded from Pugu Hills (Howell 1981). There are no fewer than 12 endemic plants (Howell 1981), although in another account the figure is seven species and one subspecies (Hawthorne 1985); one of them, *Stephanostoma stenocarpum*, is in a monotypic genus and has recently been seen in coastal bush near Dar es Salaam airport (near Pugu) (J. C. Lovett *in litt.* 1987). The small area of remaining forest is being cut down for exotic plantations, subsistence agriculture and charcoal production; there is also a danger that the mining of kaolin, currently only a small-scale operation, will be expanded and pose a serious threat to much of the forest (Howell 1981, Hawthorne 1985, SNS). Illegal felling of valuable *Chlorophora* trees was taking place in December 1986 (K. M. Howell *in litt.* 1987). All clearance in Pugu Hills should be stopped at once by the declaration of the area as a nature reserve; tree-planting schemes are needed on the periphery to allow some fuel and constructional material for local human populations (Hawthorne 1985).

38. Uluguru Mountains (Tanzania)   7°10'S 37°40'E

These lie in the Morogoro region of eastern Tanzania, just to the south of Morogoro town. The northern part of the mountains consists of a very steep, sharp, rugged ridge, running roughly north–south and reaching its highest point at Magari (2,360 m); to the south is the higher, steeply scarped Lukwangule Plateau at around 2,400 m, rising to 2,668 m at Kimhandu (Scharff *et al.* 1981, Stuart and Jensen 1985). The mountains consist mainly of precambrian metamorphic rocks, probably uplifted during the early Tertiary (Scharff *et al.* 1981, Stuart and Jensen 1985). The forest vegetation is as follows: lowland forest occurs in the eastern foothills below 500 m, now only in a few patches such as Kimboza, and is dominated by *Ficus, Chlorophora excelsa, Antiaris toxicaria, Celtis wightii, Albizia gummifera, Parkia filicoidea, Khaya nyasica* and *Sterculia appendiculata*; a drier, semi-evergreen forest once occurred on the eastern slopes between 500 and 800 m but this is now largely cleared; between 800 and 1,500 m the climax vegetation is submontane rainforest with a canopy height of 30-50 m and with giant trees heavily loaded with epiphytes, canopy dominants including *Parinari excelsa, Myrianthus holstii, Albizia gummifera, Newtonia buchananii, Allanblackia stuhlmannii* and *Ocotea usambarensis*; above 1,500 m on the eastern slopes the submontane forest gradually gives way to montane forest with a canopy of 10-30 m consisting of *Podocarpus latifolius, Ocotea usambarensis, Afrocrania volkensii, Ficalhoa laurifolia* and *Cussonia spicata*; montane mossy forest occurs on both sides of the mountain ridge above 1,850 m and is similar floristically to montane forest but also includes *Rapanea melanophloeos, Podocarpus henkelii, Schefflera myriantha, Rauvolfia volkensii* and *Balthasaria schliebenii*; on the highest peaks, above 2,100 m in the north and 2,400 m in the south, subalpine elfin forest grows, in which trees and shrubs reach only 3-6 m in height, dominant species including *Syzygium parvulum, Allanblackia ulugurensis, Podocarpus latifolius, Cussonia lukwangulensis, Polyscias stuhlmannii* and *Garcinia volkensii*; the western slopes of the mountains are drier and below 1,850 m the forest is of a scrubbier nature, extending down to 1,400 m in the north and 1,900 m in the south, while on the eastern slopes forest extends down to 800-1,500 m with scattered patches as low as 250 m; in some places, notably the Lukwangule Plateau, bamboo *Arundinaria alpina* thickets occur (Pócs 1976b, SNS). On the eastern slopes annual rainfall ranges from 1,300 to over 3,000 mm, being especially heavy at higher altitudes; on the western slopes it is drier with 800-2,000 mm per year and a dry season of 2-5 months, mainly from June to September (Pócs 1974, 1976a). Temperatures decline with altitude and frosts sometimes occur on the highest peaks (Pócs 1974, 1976b). Probably an area of about 120 sq km of forest survives in the Uluguru Mountains, including the foothills, almost all of which is included in forest reserves (SNS).

The Uluguru Bush-shrike *Malaconotus alius* (R) is endemic to the Ulugurus' forests, which also hold Mrs Moreau's Warbler *Bathmocercus winifredae* (R), Banded Green Sunbird *Anthreptes rubritorques* (R) and Tanzanian Mountain Weaver *Ploceus nicolli* (R), plus the near-threatened Southern Banded Snake Eagle *Circaetus fasciolatus*, White-winged Apalis *Apalis chariessa*, Uluguru Violet-backed Sunbird *Anthreptes neglectus* and Loveridge's Sunbird *Nectarinia loveridgei*, this last being endemic. There are four mammals endemic to the Ulugurus, the Uluguru Golden Mole *Chlorotalpa tropicalis*, the shrews *Crocidura maurisca geata* and *C. telfordi*, and the Tree Hyrax *Dendrohyrax validus schusteri*; Leopards *Panthera pardus* (V) also occur (Scharff *et al.* 1981, Hutterer 1986), as does Abbott's Duiker *Cephalophus spadix* (K) (East 1988). There are seven endemic reptiles, *Lygodactylus williamsi*, *L. schefferi uluguruensis*, *Scelotes uluguruensis*, *Typhlops uluguruensis*, *Geodipsas procterae*, *Prosymna ornatissima*, and *Chamaeleo fischeri uluguruensis* (Scharff *et al.* 1981). There are eight endemic amphibians, *Boulengerula uluguruensis*, *Scolecomorphus attenuatus*, *S. kirkii uluguruensis*, *Nectophrynoides cryptus*, *N. minutus*, *Holophryne uluguruensis*, *Probreviceps uluguruensis* and *P. macrodactylus loveridgei* (Scharff *et al.* 1981). There is also a large number of endemic invertebrates (see Scharff *et al.* 1981) and plants, including *Allanblackia ulugurensis*, *Alsophila schliebenii*, *Saintpaulia goetzeana*, *S. inconspicua* and *S. pusilla* (Pócs 1976b, Johansson 1978); Brenan (1978) lists the genera *Adenoplusia*, *Dionychastrum*, *Pseudonesohedyotis* and *Rhipidantha* as endemic to the Ulugurus.

The lower altitude forests below about 1,200 m are being cleared for cultivation, building poles, firewood and timber, and the Kimboza Forest in the foothills is particularly seriously threatened (Scharff *et al.* 1981, Rodgers *et al.* 1983). The human population density in the lower parts of the mountains is very high (Scharff *et al.* 1981). The forests of the higher parts of the mountains are on precipitous terrain and are not immediately threatened (SNS). The planting of exotic species of tree around the forests to reduce demand for natural forest wood, and the upgrading of some areas of forest to strict nature reserves, have been recommended (Scharff *et al.* 1981). Similar but more detailed proposals have been put forward for the conservation of Kimboza Forest (Rodgers *et al.* 1983) and are under consideration (Lovett 1985).

39. Uzungwa Mountains (Tanzania)   8°20'S 35°50'E
These extend approximately 200 km north-east/south-west in south-central Tanzania south of the Great Ruaha River and north of the Tazara (Great Uhuru) Railway. The mountains form a steep south-east facing escarpment rising from 300 m to 2,576 m at Luhombero with many other peaks throughout their length over 2,000 m, while to the north-west a series of rolling hills and plateaus extends down to around 300 m (Rodgers and Homewood 1982b). They were formed by the fusion of gneiss and granites, followed by uplift and faulting, and have entisol sandy soils on the plateau and oxisol sandy loam on the escarpment (Rodgers and Homewood 1982b). Wet forest extends along much of the south-east facing scarp, with drier patches on the plateau; important areas of the former type are (north-east to south-west) Mwanihana (and adjacent lowland Magombera), Matundu, Iyondo, and Uzungwa Scarp (including Chita), of the latter Image, Kisinga Rugaro, Dabaga, Mufindi Scarp, and Kibao (SNS; see map in Rodgers and Homewood 1982b). At Mwanihana three broad forest-types are recognisable: lower rainforest (400-750 m) with high tree species diversity, closed canopy at 15-25 m, and common constituents being *Erythrophleum suaveolens*, *Dialium*

holstii, *Parkia filicoidea*, *Albizia gummifera*, *Xylopia parviflora* and *Isoberlinia scheffleri*, with *Parkia* and formerly *Chlorophora* common; intermediate rainforest (750-1,250 m) with canopy (50 m) dominants being *Parinari* and *Newtonia*, occasional stands of *Cephalosphaera*, *Strombosia* and *Uapaca palludosa*, and complex layers of underwood and shrub; and montane forest (1,250 m upwards) with *Allanblackia*, *Syzygium*, *Parinari* and *Newtonia* giving way at higher levels to *Olea*, *Rapanea* and *Ocotea*, canopy varying from 15 to 40 m (Rogers and Homewood 1982b). At Chita, forest appears somewhat poorer (lower tree density, less impressive canopy) than Mwanihana (though more secure), with *Brachystegia microphylla*, *Lettowianthus stellatus* and *Vitex doniana* dominant and *Erythrophleum suaveolens*, *Tabernaemontana*, *Pachystela brevipes*, *Ficus*, *Parinari excelsa*, *Chlorophora excelsa*, *Khaya nyasica* and *Chrysophyllum* common, while *Parinari*, *Chrysophyllum*, *Newtonia*, *Albizia* and *Macaranga* are dominant at the top of the Uzungwa scarp at around 1,600 m (Rodgers and Homewood 1982b). At Mufindi (dry plateau forest), canopy height is c.20 m, dominated by *Macaranga capensis*, *Rapanea melanophloeos* and *Olinia rochetiana*, the vegetation generally very dense (van der Willigen and Lovett 1981). Mean annual rainfall along the south-east scarp is 1,800-2,000 mm, somewhat lower (1,500 mm) at Magombera, and much lower on the plateau (e.g. Iringa, 660 mm), with a pronounced rainy season from November to May (Rodgers and Homewood 1982b; also Rodgers *et al.* 1979); there are no temperature data. Some 450 sq km of the mountains are forested, the great majority being in forest reserves (Rodgers and Homewood 1982b).

Seven threatened bird species occur in the Uzungwas, of which one, the Rufous-winged Sunbird *Nectarinia rufipennis* (R), is endemic (known only from Mwanihana), the others being Swynnerton's Forest Robin *Swynnertonia swynnertoni* (R), Dappled Mountain Robin *Modulatrix orostruthus* (R), Iringa Ground Robin *Dryocichloides lowei* (R), Mrs Moreau's Warbler *Bathmocercus winifredae* (R), Banded Green Sunbird *Anthreptes rubritorques* (R) and Tanzanian Mountain Weaver *Ploceus nicolli* (R). The mountain forests also hold the near-threatened Southern Banded Snake Eagle *Circaetus fasciolatus*, White-winged Apalis *Apalis chariessa*, Uluguru Violet-backed Sunbird *Anthreptes neglectus*, Moreau's Sunbird *Nectarinia moreaui* and the Iringa Thick-billed Seed-eater *Serinus (burtoni) melanochrous*. The Uhehe Red Colobus *Colobus badius gordonorum* (E) and an undescribed race of the Crested Mangabey *Cercopithecus galeritus* occur in Magombera and the escarpment forests (Rodgers *et al.* 1980, Homewood and Rodgers 1981, Rodgers 1981). Abbott's Duiker *Cephalophus spadix* (K) is also present (East 1988). Some interesting reptiles and amphibians occur, including a gecko *Cnemaspis uzungwae*, a frog *Phlyctimantis keithae*, an unnamed tree-frog *Hyperolius* and a new species of toad *Nectophrynoides*, all of which are endemic to the forests (Rodgers *et al.* 1979, Schiøtz 1981, K. M. Howell *in litt.* 1987). Invertebrates are poorly known but endemism appears very high, e.g. species of spider in the family Linyphiidae in Mwanihana are up to 62 percent endemic (Lovett and Lovett 1985). Several species of tree appear endemic or near-endemic to Magombera, such as *Polyalthia* sp., a new species of *Ixora*, *Memecylon magnifoliatum*, *Isolona* sp. and *Isoberlinia* sp. (Rodgers and Homewood 1982b; sample species with restricted distributions are given by Lovett and Lovett 1985).

Wet forest at Mwanihana and on the Uzungwa escarpment has suffered some logging and encroachment but is considered relatively secure, both being proposed national parks in Rodgers and Homewood (1982b); however, the proposal for the latter has been rejected (SNS) while that for Mwanihana has been accepted in principle, and now only awaits some initial development funding, which is currently being sought by IUCN. However, there are some fears that expansions to the Mangula Sawmill at the foot of the mountains might signify plans to exploit the forests heavily for timber, 400 sq km of which can be considered "extractable" (J. C. Lovett verbally 1985). A further extension of the area should be considered to include the Matundu forest reserve and the southern side of the Ruaha Gorge with its baobab–euphorbia woodland (SNS). Dry forest on the Mufindi Scarp is threatened by logging, pole and liana removal, and encroachment (Rodgers and Homewood 1982b), but attempts to conserve forest on the Mufindi tea estate are being made (SNS); dry forest at Image is in good condition (Rodgers and Homewood 1982b). Of all the forest (both wet and dry) in the Uzungwas, only Mwanihana, Dabaga and Mufindi are reasonably well studied: all the remainder require substantial further investigation. The Uzungwas have a very high score of 29 and rank 9th among the forests considered in this review.

40. Southern Highlands (Tanzania)   Mdandu: 9°09'S 34°42'E
The Southern Highlands are a large area of plateau to the north of Lake Nyasa in south-west Tanzania. The highest point, Mount Rungwe, is an extinct volcano, 2,961 m. Dry montane forest exists in patches in several places in the plateau grasslands on the central and eastern side of the range, the most well known ornithologically being that at Mdandu. Wetter, much more extensive forest exists in the western part of the Highlands, the best studied being that on Mount Rungwe (SNS).

The Iringa Ground-robin *Dryocichloides lowei* (R) and the Iringa Thick-billed Seed-eater *Serinus (burtoni) melanochrous* (n-t) occur in some of the Southern Highlands forests.

Threats to the forest patches of the Southern Highlands are unknown. Further survey work is needed to assess the conservation importance of and threats to this area.

41. Mount Namuli (Mozambique)   15°21'S 37°02'E
The Namuli massif lies in north-western Mozambique, roughly rectangular in shape, very steep on its northern face (where the twin Namuli peaks rise to 2,680 and 2,650 m respectively) and longer western flank, but with a succession of buttress slopes radiating down from the western heights intersected by deep ravines on the eastern and southern sides, though these latter also have steep cliffs (Vincent 1933, 1933-1934). Dense rainforest occurred in the early 1930s in these ravines and in two large shelving areas, Ukusini and Ukalini, which straddle the parallel Nanchini and Natchuko Rivers that drain eastwards from under the two main peaks (Vincent 1933). A characteristic tree of these forests is the buttress-based *Newtonia buchananii* (= *Piptadenia africana*), reaching 30 m in height; a common creeper on larger trees is *Dalbergia arbutifolia*, whilst the undergrowth is dominated by a *Vernonia* (Vincent 1933-1934). Mean annual rainfall is in the region of 2,800-3,000 mm, and though there is a dry season in the surrounding areas from May to October the rains evidently extend intermittently throughout the year on Namuli itself; there are no temperature data, but the mountain becomes "bitterly cold" in July (Vincent 1933).

The Dappled Mountain Robin *Modulatrix orostruthus* (R) was first described from Mount Namuli, which also holds the Thyolo Alethe *Alethe choloensis* (E), the Thyolo Green Barbet *Stactolaema (olivacea) belcheri* (n-t) and the Namuli

Apalis *Apalis (thoracica) lynesi* (n-t). The mountain is the principal watershed of northern Mozambique (Vincent 1933-1934).

A tea plantation was newly established at Gurue at the southern end of Mount Namuli in the early 1930s (Vincent 1933) and presumably others would have been started in later years, leading to the loss of much lowland forest. However, at that time Namuli was wholly uninhabited by people above 900 m (Vincent 1933). Obviously the primary need is for a thorough new survey of the mountain and its forests.

42. Mount Chiradzulu (Lisau) (Malawi)   15°41'S 35°09'E

Mount Chiradzulu and the associated rocky hill, Lisau (the two are linked by a narrow saddle extending from the south-west flank of the former), lie c.20 km north-west of Blantyre and Limbe in southern Malawi, and form a central part of the "Shire Highlands" (Chapman and White 1970). The mountain, a syenitic intrusion and high plateau remnant, rises to 1,775 m and holds 150 ha of submontane evergreen forest (from 1,450 m upwards) (Dowsett-Lemaire and Dowsett in prep.). The saddle holds 150 ha of luxuriant mid-altitude forest lying at 1,300-1,450 m (on the south side of the ridge) and is characterised by *Khaya nyasica*, *Chrysophyllum gorungosanum* (reaching 30 and 24 m respectively), *Albizia gummifera* and strangler figs *Ficus* (Chapman and White 1970). Chiradzulu and Lisau, along with the Blantyre-Limbe hills (e.g. Soche) and Thyolo, attract the highest rainfall in the Shire Highlands; mean annual temperature in the Shire Highlands lies between 18.3 and 21°C (Chapman and White 1970). Chiradzulu/Lisau is a protection forest reserve (DS 1978).

The Thyolo Alethe *Alethe choloensis* (E) and Spotted Ground-thrush *Turdus fischeri* (R) occur on Chiradzulu, which also harbours the largest population in Malawi of the White-winged Apalis *Apalis chariessa* (n-t).

Chiradzulu and Lisau are threatened by illegal felling (Dowsett-Lemaire and Dowsett in prep.). Recognition of the value of the forest in water catchment, better policing of the reserve through an increase in guards, and nearby reafforestation with fast-growing exotics to meet the pressing local demand for timber are all needed (Dowsett-Lemaire and Dowsett in prep.).

43. Mount Soche (Malawi) 15°47'S 35°00'E

Mount Soche lies immediately to the south of Blantyre in southern Malawi, and forms part of the "Shire Highlands". It rises abruptly to 1,533 m and holds 150 ha of mid-altitude evergreen forest above 1,300 m (Dowsett-Lemaire and Dowsett in prep.), the floristic composition (*contra* Chapman and White 1970) being somewhat dissimilar to that on Lisau (q.v. under Mount Chiradzulu): *Chrysophyllum*, *Drypetes gerrardii* and strangling figs are important (F. Dowsett-Lemaire and R. J. Dowsett *in litt.* 1987). At Bvumbwe, 1,226 m, a little to the south, mean annual rainfall is 1,247 mm, only 110 mm of which falls in the dry season (apparently May to September); mean annual temperature is 19.2°C (Chapman and White 1970). Mount Soche is a protection forest reserve (DS 1978).

The Thyolo Alethe *Alethe choloensis* (E) and Spotted Ground-thrush *Turdus fischeri* (R) breed on Soche, which also harbours the White-winged Apalis *Apalis chariessa* (n-t) (F. Dowsett-Lemaire and R. J. Dowsett *in litt.* 1987). The small tree *Buxus nyasica*, common in the understorey on the forest ridge, is endemic to Soche (F. Dowsett-Lemaire and R. J. Dowsett *in litt.* 1987).

Soche is threatened by illegal felling and, as with Chiradzulu, the forest's value for water catchment (important for Blantyre), better policing and nearby reafforestation all need promotion locally; moreover, Soche has considerable potential as an environmental education area (Dowsett-Lemaire and Dowsett in prep.).

44. Mount Mulanje (Malawi) 16°00'S 35°35'E
Mount Mulanje, in the southern corner of easternmost Malawi, reaches 3,001 m, the highest point in tropical southern Africa: it has the form of a roughly square, sheer-sided, flat-topped massif, with a number of higher peaks flanked by dissected grassy plateaus and shelves, and with forest patches on slopes, in valleys, along streams and in sheltered hollows (Belcher 1925, Dixey 1927, Edwards 1985, IUCN 1986, Dowsett-Lemaire and Dowsett in prep.). The massif is a large syenitic intrusion (with no evidence of former volcanic activity), uplifted, faulted and considerably eroded; this erosion has left the soils (ferralitic latosols) relatively poor, a few inches deep on the plateaus though much thicker in ravines and gullies (Dixey 1927, Chapman and White 1970). On the plateaus submontane and montane forests, which together cover 4,600 ha, lie at 1,500-1,850 m and 1,850-2,300 m respectively, this being dominated locally (apparently as a fire sub-climax) by the cypress ("Mulanje Cedar") *Widdringtonia cupressoides* (the emergent *Olea capensis* is co-dominant in large areas on the Lichenya Plateau), other trees including *Cassipourea congoensis*, *Ekebergia capensis*, *Ilex mitis*, *Podocarpus latifolius* and *Polyscias fulva*; mid-altitude forest (notably on the southern slopes in Chisongeli, Ruo Gorge, the Crater), covering 1,800 ha, lies at 850-1,500 m, dominated throughout by *Newtonia buchananii*, with *Chrysophyllum gorungosanum*, *Parinari excelsa* and *Strombosia scheffleri* as important tall trees; and lowland forest extends from 600 to 850 m but now covers only about 200 ha (Dowsett-Lemaire and Dowsett in prep., F. Dowsett-Lemaire and R. J. Dowsett *in litt.* 1987). Annual rainfall is around 2,800 mm, up to 3,100 mm on the Lichenya Plateau, the main rainy season being from the end of November to the end of March, maximum around December, though in the mountains rain may fall intermittently throughout the year, on very rare occasions as hail or snow (Dixey 1927, Vincent 1933-1934; "mean annual temperature falls below 15.6°C" (Chapman and White 1970). Mount Mulanje is a protection forest reserve (DS 1978) but the lower limits are badly encroached upon (F. Dowsett-Lemaire and R. J. Dowsett *in litt.* 1987).

The Thyolo Alethe *Alethe choloensis* (E) and the Spotted Ground-thrush *Turdus fischeri* (R) occur on Mulanje, which also harbours the White-winged Apalis *Apalis chariessa* (n-t). The mountain holds the largest number of forest butterfly species in Malawi (118), of which three, *Baliochila woodi*, *Charaxes margaretae* and *Cymothoe melanjae* (R), are wholly endemic to it and may be threatened by forest destruction. There are about 30 plants endemic to the mountain, but only a proportion are forest species, including two *Streptocarpus* lithophytes, the tree *Dasylepis* (now *Rawsonia*) *burtt-davyi* (which occurs throughout mid-altitude and plateau forests), the cycad *Encephalartos gratus*, and an orchid *Polystachya*; the fern flora is the richest in Malawi (over 100 species) and one recently collected *Elaphoglossum* appears new to science (Dowsett-Lemaire and Dowsett in prep.; also Edwards 1985, IUCN 1986). The *Widdringtonia* cypresses, here at the northernmost point of their natural range, are remarkable for attaining heights of over 40 m, although elsewhere they rarely reach above 15 m (Chapman and White 1970, Edwards 1985, IUCN 1986).

The lowland and mid-altitude forests are severely threatened by clearance for subsistence cultivation and timber, e.g. Chisongeli on the south-eastern slopes was the largest tract of forest in Malawi in 1974, when it extended from 1,800 m down to 900 m, but it is now almost totally destroyed below 1,500 m (Dowsett-Lemaire and Dowsett in prep.). As with Chiradzulu, the forests' value for water catchment (vital for the tea-estates below), better policing and nearby reafforestation all need promotion locally; moreover, tea-workers should be provided with maize meal rations to prevent them destroying forest to make gardens (Dowsett-Lemaire and Dowsett in prep.). Fire threatens forest patches although efforts are made to control its effects on the plateaus; certain vigorous exotic plants are invading and altering the communities and require control; bauxite deposits remain to be exploited on the western side of the mountain at 1,800-1,900 m (Dixey 1927, IUCN 1986); that tourism could become unmanageable if (e.g.) a road were built to provide easy access to higher areas (IUCN 1986) is not considered a serious threat, and indeed a road could give forest staff better mobility for fire- and poacher-control; meanwhile, refugees from Mozambique are invading the eastern slopes in escalating numbers (F. Dowsett-Lemaire and R. J. Dowsett *in litt.* 1987).

45. Mount Thyolo (Malawi)   16°02'S 35°05'E
Mount Thyolo lies c.30 km south of Blantyre in southern Malawi, and forms the southernmost part of the "Shire Highlands". It rises to 1,464 m and comprises a long ridge falling very steeply in the west to the Shire valley; soil is acidic sand and clay, high in phosphorus (Chapman and White 1970). There is mid-altitude evergreen forest from the summit down to 1,200 m, dominated by strangling figs (especially *Ficus sansibarica*, also *F. natalensis* and *F. kirkii*), and with many lianas, mosses and epiphytes, canopy height 18-36 m and a fairly thick ground vegetation; *Khaya nyasica* lowland forest occurs in gullies at 900-1,100 m scattered throughout adjacent tea-estates (F. Dowsett-Lemaire and R. J. Dowsett *in litt.* 1987; also Chapman and White 1970, Johnston-Stewart 1977, 1982). Mean annual rainfall at Thyolo Boma (902 m) is 1,327 mm, mostly falling in the rainy season from November to March; mean annual temperature at Thyolo Boma is 20.8°C (Chapman and White 1970). There are 10 sq km of mid-altitude forest, extending along the ridge for up to 6 km and over 1 km wide, and a further 6 sq km of lowland forest (Dowsett-Lemaire and Dowsett in prep; also Chapman and White 1970). The mid-altitude forest is a protection forest reserve (DS 1978).

The Thyolo Alethe *Alethe choloensis* (E) and Spotted Ground-thrush *Turdus fischeri* (R) occur on Thyolo, as do the Thyolo Green Barbet *Stactolaema (olivacea) belcheri* (n-t) and White-winged Apalis *Apalis chariessa* (n-t) (see Johnston-Stewart 1977, 1982). The mountain is also important as the only locality in Malawi for Delegorgue's Pigeon *Columba delegorguei* and for holding the larger of two Malawi populations of the Green-headed Oriole *Oriolus chlorocephalus* (Dowsett-Lemaire and Dowsett in prep.).

Considerable illegal felling has occurred on the north side of Thyolo and, as with Chiradzulu, the forest's value for water catchment (important to prevent the Nsuadzi River becoming a seasonal flood), better policing and nearby reafforestation (to compensate for the loss of the natural *Brachystegia* buffer-zone) all need promotion locally (Dowsett-Lemaire and Dowsett in prep.; also Johnston-Stewart 1982).

46. Mount Chiperone   (Mozambique)   16°30'S 35°44'E
This isolated peak is situated in western Mozambique some 60 km south of
Mount Mulanje in Malawi, and rises to 2,180 m (Benson 1950). Forest-type is
presumably similar to that of similar mountains in southern Malawi, Chiperone
being close enough to that country to give its name to a dry season rainy mist
that blows from its direction (see Chapman and White 1970), but there is no
detailed information.

The Thyolo Alethe *Alethe choloensis* (E) and White-winged Apalis *Apalis
chariessa* (n-t) are recorded from Mount Chiperone.

Nothing is known of the condition of forest on Chiperone today. The almost
total lack of exploration – zoological, botanical or otherwise – on the mountain
obviously requires correction (the birds above being recorded during a mere
week's survey).

47. Gorongosa Mountain   (Mozambique)   18°30'S 34°03'E
This mountain lies in western Mozambique 115 km east of the Inyanga Highlands
in Zimbabwe, and rises to 1,863 m (Mount Gogôgo), on the eastern edge of the
Manica Platform (Irwin 1979). It is oval in shape, 30 km from north to south
and 20 km from east to west, an isolated, erosional remnant of "eruptive"
formation, essentially granitic and gabbroid (Pinto 1959, Tinley undated a). Apart
from montane grasslands on the summit plateaus (Tinley undated a), it is (or was)
almost entirely covered in primary forest, with patches of subalpine evergreen
forest at around 1,800 m dominated by *Podocarpus*, *Widdringtonia* and *Philippia*,
very wet montane forest from 1,000 to 1,600 m dominated by *Aphloia*, *Maesa*,
etc., and with floristically similar but much patchier forest below 1,000 m (Pinto
1959). Annual rainfall is over 2,000 mm (Tinley undated a). Although surveys
in the 1960s recommended that the greater part of the mountain should lie within
the Gorongosa National Park (Tinley undated a), none of it does so (J. Burlison
in litt. 1983).

Swynnerton's Forest Robin *Swynnertonia swynnertoni* (R) and the Chirinda
Apalis *Apalis chirindensis* (n-t) occur on Gorongosa. The forest is described as "of
great botanical interest" (Pinto 1959).

Forest clearance in the form of shifting cultivation (encroaching upwards) is a
chronic problem; the government has tried to limit local people to below the
600 m contour but enforcement has been difficult while the mountain remains a
main base for insurgents (J. Burlison *in litt.* 1983). The perennial waters rising
on Gorongosa Mountain are essential to the maintenance of the ecosystems of the
Gorongosa National Park, hence the imperative of including the mountain with the
park boundaries (Tinley undated a).

48. Vumba Highlands   (Zimbabwe)   19°07'S 32°46'E
These lie just south of Mutare in the central part of the Eastern Highlands of
Zimbabwe, close to the Mozambique border (see map in Irwin 1979; also
Masterson 1985). Numerous discontinuous relic patches of closed evergreen forest
survive on private land where the ground is too steep or rocky for cultivation; the
altitude is from 1,200 to 1,600 m with rainfall over 1,000 m per annum (G. E.
Grout *in litt.* 1987). Two areas of forest in the Vumba Highlands are protected
by legislation, these being the Bunga Forest Botanical Reserve (495 ha) and the
Vumba Botanical Reserve (42 ha) which is within the Vumba Botanical Gardens
(201 ha) (Robertson 1986, G. E. Grout *in litt.* 1987). The Bunga Forest contains
80 ha of forest dominated by *Syzygium guineense* (Robertson 1986).

Swynnerton's Forest Robin *Swynnertonia swynnertoni* (R), Forest Prinia *Prinia robertsi* (n-t) and Chirinda Apalis *Apalis chirindensis* (n-t) occur in the Vumba Highlands forests.

Annual grass fires are a serious threat to the survival of some of the forest patches in the Vumba Highlands, including the Bunga Forest Botanical Reserve (Robertson 1986, G. E. Grout *in litt.* 1987). A protective measure would be to burn annually a belt of grassland around the perimeter of the forests in the early dry season so that late fires do not reach the forest edge (G. E. Grout *in litt.* 1987). Such a management policy is already carried out at Bunga Forest (Robertson 1986).

49. Chirinda Forest (Zimbabwe)   20°25'S 34°44'E

This forest lies c.33 km south of Chipinge in the southern extremity of the Eastern Highlands of Zimbabwe, close to the Mozambique border (Banks 1976). Forest vegetation is confined to the highly fertile dolerite caps and ranges from 1,067 m to 1,250 m (Banks 1976) although the forest-dependent Swynnerton's Forest Robin *Swynnertonia swynnertoni* is recorded at Chirinda from 900 to 1,200 m (Irwin 1981). Chirinda is mid-altitude closed evergreen forest, a rich and varied habitat with very large trees including *Khaya nyasica*, *Lovoa swynnertoni*, *Strychnos*, *Diospyros*, *Chrysophyllum gorungosanum*, *Craibia brevicaudata* and *Ficus chirindensis*, sometimes as much as 60 m high, with a dense undergrowth of shrubs and saplings including *Dracaena fragrans* (Swynnerton 1907, Irwin 1981, R. du Toit *in litt.* 1987). Mean annual rainfall is 1,381 mm with wide annual variations; the climate is mild and frosts are unknown (Banks 1976). The forested area is 6 sq km (606 ha) and lies within a protected area of 9.5 sq km, this being both a forest and a botanical reserve (Banks 1976).

Swynnerton's Forest Robin *Swynnertonia swynnertoni* (R), Forest Prinia *Prinia robertsi* (n-t) and Chirinda Apalis *Apalis chirindensis* (n-t) occur in Chirinda Forest. The Silinda Rat *Aethomys silindensis* is known from Chirinda Forest and two other localities, and Leopards *Panthera pardus* (V) have been recorded there (Smithers 1976, 1983). Certain reptiles are evidently potentially at risk, such as Marshall's Dwarf Chameleon *Rhampholeon marshalli* and the amphisbaenian *Chirindia swynnertoni*, both restricted to the Eastern Highlands and (in the latter case) adjacent Mozambique (Broadley 1976). The Forest Green Butterfly *Euryphera achlyus* is known only from Chirinda Forest and Ngoye Forest, South Africa (q.v.) (Huntley 1965). The Chirinda Forest has many endemic molluscs and other invertebrates (A. C. van Bruggen *in litt.* to S. M. Wells, 1981), and is the type-locality for many trees, some of which are restricted in Zimbabwe to Chirinda alone (Goldsmith 1976).

Felling and exploitation have been prevented since 1939 and the only but permanent threat to the forest must be the very small size it now has, although there have been attempts to extend its area through planting up fringes with indigenous trees (Banks 1976), though these efforts are not thought to be of significance for the survival of the forest (R. du Toit *in litt.* 1987). Chirinda Forest is protected by legislation in the Forestry Act and the Parks and Wildlife Act (G. E. Grout *in litt.* 1987).

50. Coastal forests in Sofala, Mozambique

Several small forest patches exist along the coast of Mozambique, south of the Zambezi River. The exact sites of importance for forest bird conservation are not yet clear, and should be the subject of further survey work, but it is certain that some exist on the Cheringoma coast between Beira and the Zambezi estuary, notably at Dondo (=Mzimbiti) and the Inhamitanda (Inhamitanga) Forest, and possibly at Marromeu, all in Sofala province (J. Burlison *in litt.* 1983). Annual rainfall at Beira averages over 1,400 mm, most falling from December to March (Tinley undated b). The moist evergreen forest patches of the Cheringoma coast are composed of *Pteleopsis myrthifolia*, *Erythrophloeum suaveolens*, *Hirtella zanguebarica*, *Pachystela brevipes*, *Chlorophora exelsa* and others (Tinley undated a). None is apparently protected.

The East Coast Akalat *Sheppardia gunningi* (R) occurs in these forests, as do three near-threatened species: Southern Banded Snake Eagle *Circaetus fasciolatus*; Rudd's Apalis *Apalis ruddi* and Woodward's Batis *Batis fratrum*. Three non-forest near-threatened species, Neergaard's Sunbird *Nectarinia neergaardi*, Lemon-breasted Canary *Serinus citrinipectus* and Pink-throated Twinspot *Hypargos margaritatus*, are also known from the general area of coastal southern Mozambique.

Considerable forest exploitation and shifting cultivation are threatening the Inhamitanda Forest (J. Burlison *in litt.* 1983). Fieldwork is urgently needed to determine the conservation problems and requirements of these rare forest birds and their habitats. A representative sample of the moist evergreen forest of the Cheringoma coast could be protected if the proposed coastward extension of the Gorongosa National Park, the Chiniziua Enclave, were to be proclaimed (Tinley undated a).

ANGOLA SCARP

This short section treats the distinctive and unusual forests of western Angola. As is clear from the text, the detailed conservation requirements of the area are not at all well known and more survey work is needed to identify the exact sites which merit conservation. The conservation requirements of these areas have been discussed briefly by Huntley (1974a,b, 1978) and Dowsett (1985). In this review we identify two areas of particular importance for forest bird conservation in the region:

No.	Forest area	Priority score	Position among all the forests in this review
51	Amboim and adjacent forests, Angola	28	11=
52	Bailundu Highlands, Angola	5	63=

Details of the priority scores and how they are calculated are given in the introductory section "Priorities for Conservation Action". There is every reason to believe that the forest patches listed above are seriously threatened and, in view of their uniqueness, action to conserve them is urgently needed. Map 1a shows the geographic locations of these areas.

51. Amboim and adjacent forests (Angola)   10°40'S 14°15'E

An extended but fragmented series of forests and forest patches exists along the Angolan escarpment from Dondo south to Quilenges: apparently the largest and perhaps the most important is the so-called "Amboim forest", immediately north of Gabela and stretching across the Amboim hinterland (as described by Hall 1960 and mapped in Barbosa 1970). The forests range in area from a few hectares to several thousands of hectares and form a continuum from dry scrub forest or thicket to tall moist rainforest, following a gradient of moisture availability and altitude: at the dry extreme (receiving 400 to 600 mm rainfall) a dense thicket of trees 10 to 20 m tall, including *Ceiba pentandra*, *Bombax reflexum*, *Pteleopsis myrtifolia*, *Adansonia digitata*, *Lannea welwitschii*, *Albizia glabrescens* and numerous climbers, covers the escarpment foothills from within 10 km of the coast south of the Cuanza river to the midslopes and most drainage lines of the steeply rising hills inland of Amboim, Novo Redondo and Lobito (fairly extensive patches of this thicket fall within the limits of Parque Nacional da Kisama) (B. J. Huntley *in litt.* 1987). Inland of the dry thicket, on the higher (400 to 1,200 m), moister (600 to 1,200 mm per annum) slopes, an increasingly luxuriant and tall (up to 40 m) forest occurs, with species such as *Bombax reflexum*, *Khaya acanthotheca*, *Blighia unijugata*, *Zanha golungensis*, *Piptadeniastrum africanum*, *Celtis mildbraedii*, *Spathodea campanulata* etc., dominating a moist cloud-forest type with abundant epiphytes but fewer lianas than the low-altitude thickets (B. J. Huntley *in litt.* 1987; also Airy Shaw 1947). These forests were extensively utilised for coffee production, the undergrowth (but not the canopy) being cleared and planted to coffee, but much of the area previously maintained for coffee production has reverted to secondary regrowth and a dense, almost impenetrable thicket has now replaced the open ground and shrub strata that characterise pristine areas of these forests (B. J. Huntley *in litt.* 1987). Rainfall data from near Dondo show a very dry period between May and September with peak precipitation in November/December (monthly mean up to 180 mm) and March/April (monthly mean up to 250 mm) (Hall 1960); all scarp forests are situated so as to be sheltered from the dry easterly June winds (Airy Shaw 1947). None of these forests appears to be protected (none is treated, e.g., in Horsten 1982).

Within the region of these ten forest patches lie the localities of Mumbondo, Assango and Conda, as well of course as Dondo, Amboim, Gabela and Vila Nova do Seles, and from these seven sites four threatened species are known, the Gabela Helmet-shrike *Prionops gabela* (I), Monteiro's Bush-shrike *Malaconotus monteiri* (I), Gabela Akalat *Sheppardia gabela* (I) and Pulitzer's Longbill *Macrosphenus pulitzeri* (I). The near-threatened Grey-striped Francolin *Francolinus griseostriatus*, Amboim Bush-shrike *Laniarius (luhderi) amboimensis*, and White-fronted Wattle-eye *Platysteira albifrons* also occur. Of the threatened species, the helmet-shrike and akalat are almost entirely restricted to the Gabela region, while Monteiro's Bush-shrike and Pulitzer's Longbill, endemic to the Angolan escarpment (if we discount a single, ancient record of the former from Mount Cameroon: q.v.), extend somewhat further to the north and south respectively. Of the near-threatened species, all are endemic to the Angola escarpment, and the bush-shrike is known only from Gabela. We have no data on other important fauna or flora; however, the factors that explain the ornithological importance of the Angolan escarpment (see Hall 1960) seem likely to have worked for speciation in other forms of life there as well.

Threats to these forest patches are currently unknown, other than that (a) undergrowth in at least some has been cleared for coffee cultivation and (b) all are so small that they are permanently vulnerable to exploitation, modification and clearance. For all four threatened bird species mentioned above urgent surveys are required to determine their status, distribution and conservation needs, with a view to recommending the establishment of reserves, but such surveys should form components of a broad-based faunal and floral investigation of the forests of the Gabela region, and that protection in the strictest degree for the largest hectarage achievable should be anticipated as the likeliest resulting recommendation of such work. A 50 sq km Gabela Strict Nature Reserve has already been proposed (Huntley 1974b) and this requires follow-up. These forests have a very high score of 28, ranking 11th= among all the forests considered in this review.

52. Bailundu Highlands (Angola),   Galanga: 12°04'S 15°09'E

Inland of the Angolan escarpment, on the highlands that rise from the interior plateau, a number of extremely small (most no greater than 20 ha) forest patches occur in sheltered sites, mainly deep ravines at 2,000-2,500 m, on Mount Môco and the Mombolo Plateau (on Mount Môco there were at least 15 patches in the early 1970s) (Huntley 1974b, B. J. Huntley *in litt.* 1987). Dominant or otherwise significant trees, 10-15 m in height, include *Pittosporum*, *Olea*, *Podocarpus milanjianus*, *Apodytes dimidiata* and *Ilex mitis*; rainfall is 1,000 to 1,300 mm per year (Huntley 1974b, B. J. Huntley *in litt.* 1987). The total area of forest on

Mount Môco was under 100 ha in the 1970s, and none of it was protected
(Huntley 1978).

Swierstra's Francolin *Francolinus swierstrai* (I) is known from Mount Môco,
Mount Soque and the Mombolo Plateau, the Fernando Po Swift *Apus sladeniae*
(K), probably not a forest species, is known from Môco, and the Black-chinned
Weaver *Ploceus nigrimentum* (K) is known from the Mombolo Plateau and
Galanga, a locality west of Soque and north of Môco (although of these only the
francolin is likely to be forest-dependent). Moreover, Margaret's Batis *Batis
margaritae* (n-t) occurs on the upper slopes of Môco. All these species have
scattered populations elsewhere; only the Francolin is endemic to the uplands of
Angola. The forests of the Bailundu Highlands differ both in structure and
phytogeographic relationships from the escarpment zone, their fauna and flora
showing Afromontane links; the biogeographic interest of these forests is immense
(Huntley 1974b).

These tiny patches of Afromontane forest are under severe threat: timber and
fuelwood extraction from them continues unabated, the people occupying the cold
and relatively treeless slopes having no alternative resource (B. J. Huntley *in litt.*
1987). Pleas for conservation action (including the proposal of a 60 sq km
Mount Môco Strict Nature Reserve) have been made in a series of reports and
papers by Huntley (1974a, 1974b, 1978) but nothing appears to have been done.
A new initiative is urgently required.

AFRICA MISCELLANEOUS

In addition to the forests of the five preceding regions, there are a few other isolated forests on the African mainland of particular importance for bird conservation. Most of these have bird species endemic to them, or virtually so. We have identified six forests (Maps 1a and 1b) in this category:

No.	Forest area	Priority score	Position among all the forests in this review
54	Day Forest, Djibouti	10	37=
56	Forests of south-western Nigeria	10	37=
53	Forests of northern Angola and western Zaïre	8	50=
55	Forests around Neghelli, Ethiopia	6	56=
57	Ngoye Forest, South Africa	5	63=
58	Daloh Forest, Somalia	4	71=

Details of the priority scores and how they are calculated are given in the introductory section "Priorities for Conservation Action".

53. Forests of northern Angola and western Zaïre
Very little is known of this area, but the area north-east of Duque de Bragança in Angola and the Bombo-Lumene Nature Reserve 500 km to the north in western Zaïre are known to be of ornithological interest.

The White-headed Robin-chat *Cossypha heinrichi* (I) is known only from this area, and there are a number of primates present, notably Black Mangabey *Cercocebus aterrimus* (K) (Oates 1986).

Very little is known of the threats to, or the conservation status of, this huge area. There is considerable evidence of timber companies planning to move into western Zaïre in the near future (Prigogine 1985).

54. Day Forest (Djibouti)   11°47'N 42°40'E
The only extensively wooded area in Djibouti, Day stands in the Goda mountains about 25 km due west of Tadjourah. The mountains (highest point 1,783 m) consist of a grey shaly rock of volcanic origin, with plateaus deeply eroded by watercourses and edged by precipitous, sparsely vegetated slopes; the forest grows on the plateaus at c.1,500 m (Welch and Welch 1984; also Vayssière and Chédeville 1960). Primary forest is dominated by juniper *Juniperus procera* (which grows to 5-8 m), with *Buxus hildebrandtii*, *Acacia etbaica*, *A. seyal* and *Clutia abyssinica* the main understorey species (Welch and Welch 1984, 1986; fuller data on flora in Chevalier 1939a,b, with vegetation map in Blot 1985). Rainfall is not high, seldom above 300 mm per year, mainly between November and March, but the forest receives additional moisture from frequent mists

(Chevalier 1939a,b, Welch and Welch 1986); it covers c.1,400 ha and lies wholly within the Day National Park (Welch and Welch 1984).

The Djibouti Francolin *Francolinus ochropectus* (E) is known chiefly from Day, although there is a relict population in a smaller and much more degraded patch of juniper at Mabla at the eastern end of the Goda mountains (Blot 1985, Welch *et al.* 1986). The wadi at Bankoualé in the northern part of Day holds not only a population of the francolin but also a significant proportion of the world's population of the threatened Bankoualé Palm *Livistona carinensis* (Welch and Welch 1984, 1986; also Lucas and Synge 1978). The whole forest is recognised as a relict of an ancient, rare and dying floral community (Chevalier 1939a).

Day, whose fragility and vulnerability were recognised nearly 50 years ago (Chevalier 1939a), is seriously threatened owing to chronic failure to achieve balanced management: fires, started deliberately to open areas for grazing, destroy not only vegetation but the fertility of the soil and thus prevent regeneration; overgrazing and trampling, chiefly by cattle, are now the main problem; firewood-gathering results in the shipment of seven tons daily to Djibouti city; climatic changes that result from all these activities also have a perceptible adverse effect on the forest's dynamics; human disturbance (by the 2,000 local people, plus the French Army in summer and an unknown number of tourists) may have certain deleterious effects; and there are plans to introduce agricultural and residential schemes to the forest, which could have several serious consequences, notably through the diversion of water for irrigation and domestic purposes (Welch and Welch 1984, 1986; also Blot 1985). At the present rate of degeneration, no primary forest will remain by 1995: measures needed to prevent further degeneration are (a) a strong local education campaign, (b) reorganisation of the local pastoral system and the creation of alternative forms of subsistence, and (c) the planting of buffering belts to reduce desiccation (Welch and Welch 1984). Hunting – which was a problem back in 1950 (Vayssière and Chédeville 1960) – must also be curbed (Blot 1985).

55. Forests around Neghelli (Ethiopia)   5°20'N 39°35'E
There is an area of forest (or forest patches) in the upper Dawa and Ganale Dorya valleys in the vicinity of Arero and Neghelli (Negele). At least part of this forest is dominated by *Juniperus procera* and is at an altitude of at least 1,800 m. One such forest at Arero covered only 25 sq km in 1941-1942, and some other patches where the species occurs are even smaller.

Prince Ruspoli's Turaco *Tauraco ruspolii* (R) is endemic to these forests.

Nothing is known of the conservation of these forests and a survey of the area is needed. There is always the possibility of the forest being cleared as a result of resettlement schemes, but there is no evidence of this.

56. Forests of south-western Nigeria
This is the lowland forested area between the Niger River and the border with Benin. There has been very heavy deforestation in this area but forest is known to survive in the Okumu Forest Reserve (1,200 sq km) in Bendel State and, probably, other areas in Ondo and Ogun States.

The Ibadan Malimbe *Malimbus ibadanensis* (E) is endemic to south-western Nigeria, as is the now critically threatened White-throated Guenon (Red-bellied Monkey) *Cercopithecus erythrogaster* (V) (Oates 1986).

The forests in south-western Nigeria are under intense pressure for timber and converting to plantations and farms, and hunting is also uncontrolled (Oates 1986).

In November 1985 and June 1986, logging was being carried out in the Okumu Forest Reserve, which is now criss-crossed with logging roads (Ash and Sharland 1986, A. A. Green verbally 1986). The future for this forest is very bleak. None of the areas from which the Ibadan Malimbe has been recorded are known to be protected, and a good many of them appear to have been destroyed (Collar and Stuart 1985). It has not been reported from the Okumu Forest, nor from any other forest reserves in the region, and a survey is needed to establish exactly where it survives. The Red-bellied Monkey is known from Okumu (Oates 1986), though it may now be exterminated there (Ash and Sharland 1986). There is an urgent need to conserve sizeable areas of forest for both species, preferably in places where they occur together.

57. Daloh Forest Reserve (Somalia)   10°45'N 47°24'E
This small forest lies on the scarp in the central part of northern Somalia, just north of Erigavo. The area is at 1,800-2,000 m and is a "rocky evergreen-forest zone" where *Juniperus procera, Olea chrysophylla, Dodonea viscosa, Cadia purpurea* and *Sideroxylon* sp. are the principal plants (Williams 1956). The total area of tree-cover must be very small; it is classified as a forest reserve, but it is not known to what extent this is safeguarding the existence of the forest (J. S. Ash *in litt.* 1986).

The Warsangli Linnet *Acanthis johannis* (R) is found in Daloh, and although it is not wholly forest-dependent Daloh appears to be the only locality at which the species is at all numerous.   The Somali Olive Thrush *Turdus (abyssinicus) ludoviciae* (n-t) is common there (Ash and Miskell 1981).

The forest at Daloh is degraded and there are many open areas (Ash and Miskell 1981). It needs to be established how rapid this degradation is and how far it has proceeded, and strict conservation of the forest seems essential. It is a spectacularly beautiful area and is worth protecting on this account alone (J. S. Ash *in litt.* 1986). A scheme to develop the area for tourism did not materialise but there have been recent reports that the area should be exploited for furniture-making and re-planted with a quick-growing exotic (J. S. Ash *in litt.* 1986). Clearly, such a scheme would be most damaging.

58. Ngoye Forest (South Africa)   28°50'S 31°42'E
This relict forest lies near the coast by Eshowe, in KwaZulu, South Africa. It is one of a series of isolated patches along the coast of south-east South Africa, all relicts of formerly much more extensive tall forest in the region. Ngoye lies on Basement Complex of two main types, biotite granite gneiss and hornblend biotite schist, most of the forest lying on the former at 300-450 m above sea-level (Huntley 1965).   Important species forming the climax forest, whose emergents reach some 25 m in height, are *Trichilia dregeana, Syzygium cordatum, Ficus natalensis, F. craterostoma, Harpephyllum caffrum, Mimusops obovota, Ekebergia capensis, Protorhus longifolia, Drypetes gerrardii, Millettia sutherlandi, Chrysophyllum viridifolium, Garcinia gerrardii* and *Podocarpus latifolius,* the shrubby undergrowth being dense and woody lianas numerous (Clancey 1964, Huntley 1965, Moll 1978, M. Lawes *in litt.* 1987).   Rainfall is in summer, 75 percent falling in October to March, with May to July largely dry (Clancey 1964); between May 1975 and April 1979, mean annual rainfall was 1,899 mm (M. Lawes *in litt.* 1987).   Mean annual temperature is 19.6°C (Huntley 1965). Ngoye Forest covers approximately 2,830 ha (Huntley 1965, M. Lawes *in litt.* 1987) and is controlled by the KwaZulu government (King 1978-1979).

The Spotted Ground-thrush *Turdus fischeri* (R) and the Ngoye Green Barbet *Stactolaema (olivacea) woodwardi* (n-t) breed in Ngoye Forest, the latter being wholly restricted to it. The Ngoye Red Squirrel *Paraxerus ornatus* and Ngoye Centipede *Cormocephalus granulosus* are endemic to the forest, and the Forest Green Butterfly *Euryphera achlyus* only otherwise occurs in Chirinda Forest, Zimbabwe (q.v.); a hemiparasitic plant, *Loranthus woodii*, is endemic to Ngoye, and the forest generally is of "great scientific importance" for the link it forms between the tropical forests of Central and Eastern Africa and the temperate and subtropical forests of Knysna and Pondoland (Huntley 1965).

The small size of Ngoye Forest is a permanent source of concern; a large amount of illegal woodcutting takes place, and cattle are grazed within the forest (Moll 1978, D. Lawson *in litt.* 1987). Trapping of mammals is taking place and most of the larger species have now been eliminated (D. Lawson *in litt.* 1987). There are also illegal cutting and burning activities (Moll 1978). R. J. Dowsett and F. Dowsett-Lemaire (*in litt.* 1987) suggest that the cattle grazing is not having a serious impact on the vegetation of the forest, and that there is no immediate cause for alarm for the two bird species. However, the implementation of a sound management plan for Ngoye Forest is urgently needed, not only for its intrinsic value but for the economic importance it retains for local people (Huntley 1965).

MADAGASCAR

The unique forests of Madagascar are of critical importance for conservation (Dee 1986, Mittermeier in prep.). Probably the most important areas are in the eastern rainforest belt of the island, though there are also some priority areas in the dry forest of the north-west and in the brush forest of the south-west. In this review we identify 11 forests of particular importance for forest bird conservation in Madagascar:

No.	Forest area	Priority score	Position among all the forests in this review
66	Sihanaka Forest	46	3
65	Périnet-Analamazaotra Faunal Reserve	44	4
69	Marojejy R.N.I. and Andapa region	26	16=
64	Ranomafana	26	16=
68	Forest around Maroantsetra	25	19=
63	Tsarafidy and Ankazomivady Forests	13	28=
67	Tsaratanana Massif	13	28=
59	Brush forest north of Tuléar	12	32=
61	Ankarafantsika R.N.I.	8	50=
60	Zombitse Forest	6	56=
62	Andohahela R. N. I.	5	63=

Details of the priority scores and how they are calculated are given in the introductory section "Priorities for Conservation Action". Map 6 shows the geographic locations of these 11 key conservation areas.

Because of the high number of threatened and near-threatened birds in Madagascar, the forest areas where they overlap may take on an exaggerated significance. However, ornithological exploration in Madagascar is very incomplete, and the areas identified below must largely reflect this problem. It seems very likely, for example, that the long, almost unbroken sleeve of rainforest extending down the eastern side of the country holds the majority of rainforest-dependent species throughout its length; there is, at any rate, no reason to suppose that the threatened forms are confined to the pockets described below. Indeed, it appears that the broadest part of this rainforest sleeve (at the latitude of Ile de Sainte-Marie) has never been explored ornithologically (this is the region where the Snail-eating Coua *Coua delalandei* might still possibly survive, and indeed where the mysterious Red-tailed Newtonia *Newtonia fanovanae* may yet be rediscovered), and the great majority of the rainforest south of the latitude of Antananarivo has suffered similar neglect; forest on the Masoala peninsula may also prove of high importance. A converse problem has been that, in the general rainforest area between Antananarivo and the coast of Tamatave, there are many forest localities where threatened birds have overlapped (e.g. Rogez, Lakato, Vohi-

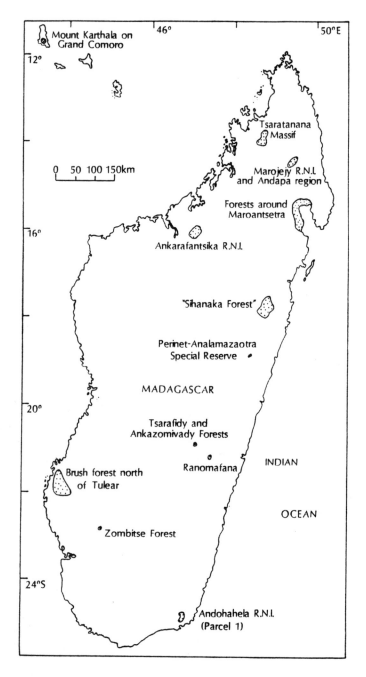

Map 6: Madagascar (with Grand Comoro)

bazaha, "East Imerina forests", the Mangoro valley at Ampasimaneva) and, as sufficient doubt exists as to their continued existence, it has been decided to omit these localities from consideration here (Rogez, now called Andekaleka, is largely deforested: M. E. Nicoll *in litt.* 1987). A further complication is that some altitudinal migration, and even possibly some north-south migration along the rainforest sleeve, may occur, so that the forest areas identified below may be insufficient to provide total insurance for some of the species they contain. Rectification of this imbalance in knowledge is called for in Collar *et al.* (1987).

59. Brush forest north of Tuléar   Lake Ihotry: 21°59'S 43°36'E

The "forest" in question lies north of Tuléar (Toliara) between the Mangoky and Fiherenana rivers in south-west Madagascar, bounded in the west by the sea and in the east by the 150 m contour. The relief is flat, the soil very sandy, the vegetation characterised as "subdesert brush", commonly featuring the cactus-like *Didierea madagascariensis* (the area in question is the northernmost extension of this type of habitat in Madagascar); mean annual rainfall is below 500 mm and mean annual temperature above 24°C (Rand 1936, Appert 1968a,b). The area of habitat may be fairly extensive but none of it is protected. White (1983) refers to the habitat as "West Malagasy deciduous thicket".

The Subdesert Mesite *Monias benschi* (R) and Long-tailed Ground-roller *Uratelornis chimaera* (R), two of Madagascar's most distinctive birds (both in monotypic genera within endemic families) are wholly restricted to this forest. The Banded Kestrel *Falco zoniventris* (n-t) might also occur in this area (R. J. Dowsett *in litt.* 1987).

A 20-year-old report that this forest is being rapidly destroyed has not been confirmed (see Collar and Stuart 1985: 353) but its vulnerability to fire and clearance must be a permanent source of concern; a study to determine the extent and type of habitat destruction in the area, with a view to identifying one or more key areas for protection, is urgently needed. Such work could double with detailed biological study of both bird species mentioned above, this being especially important for the ground-roller, whose habitat requirements are the more specialised and which apparently undertakes short-distance migrations, not yet understood.

60. Zombitse Forest   22°47'S 44°40'E

Zombitse (Zombitsy) Forest lies east of Sakaraha in south-west Madagascar, to the south of the Fiherenana river, at an altitude between 485 and 824 m; the topography consists of gently undulating hills, with sandy soils and thin humus layer; the area has no watercourses but is a major watershed (Nicoll and Langrand 1986b). The forest is dense, dry and deciduous, with lianas, the 15-20 m tall canopy being dominated by *Securinega seyrigii*, *Cedrelopsis grevii*, *Commiphora arofy*, *Khaya madagascariensis* and *Euphorbia anterophora*; mean annual rainfall is somewhat above 700 mm (dry season from May to October), mean annual temperature around 23°C (Rand 1936, Colston 1972, Nicoll and Langrand 1986b). Zombitse and related forests cover together some 1,000 sq km, the Zombitse Reserved Forest embracing some 215 sq km of this (Nicoll and Langrand 1986b), but the bird species for which it is most important is only known to inhabit 0.5 sq km.

Appert's Greenbul *Phyllastrephus apperti* (R) inhabits one small corner of Zombitse Forest, and is otherwise known from only one or two other localities. Benson's Rockthrush *Monticola bensoni* (K) has also been recorded (outside its breeding season) in the forest, although all other evidence indicates it is not a forest-dependent species. The near-threatened Madagascar Cuckoo-falcon *Aviceda madagascariensis* and Banded Kestrel *Falco zoniventris* occur (Nicoll and Langrand 1986b). The gecko *Phelsuma standingi* is confined to the region (Nicoll and Langrand 1986b) and the butterfly *Papilio grosesmithi* (R) occurs in the forest (Collins and Morris 1985).

That part of Zombitse which is a forest reserve is presumably liable to felling at any time, in addition to which the region in general is at risk from fires started by man. Control of deforestation and burning is essential for ecological stability in the region, and improved protection for Zombitse is very desirable. Fieldwork to determine better the range and status of Appert's Greenbul is also important.

61. Ankarafantsika R.N.I.   16°10'S 46°50'E

The Réserve Naturelle Intégrale de l'Ankarafantsika lies 40 km north-east of Ambato-Boény, in Majunga province, Madagascar. The area is part of a sandy (sandstone) plateau at 75-390 m, descending gently in the north and west but with a rugged relief to the east and a cliff to the south (Andriamampianina and Peyrieras 1972, Jenkins 1987). The forest is dense, dry, and deciduous, containing about 170 species of tree and shrub in 35 families, including *Dalbergia*, *Commiphora*, *Hildegardia*, and numerous Leguminosae and Myrtaceae, with many lianas and generally a fairly dense undergrowth, but virtually no epiphytes; annual rainfall lies between 1,000 and 1,500 mm, with a marked dry season from May to November, and mean annual temperature is around 26°C (17-35°C) (Andriamampianina and Peyrieras 1972, Jenkins 1987). The area of the R.N.I. (Strict Nature Reserve) is 602 sq km and borders a nature reserve of 200-300 sq km to the west (Jenkins 1987).

The White-breasted Mesite *Mesitornis variegata* (R) and Van Dam's Vanga *Xenopirostris damii* (R) occur at Ankarafantsika, the latter being known from only one other (old) site in the country, the former now known from a handful of other localities (Appert 1985, *BBC Wildlife* 4 [1986] 662-663). The Madagascar Little Grebe *Tachybaptus pelzelnii* (K) and Madagascar Fish Eagle *Haliaeetus vociferoides* (E) are also recorded from the R.N.I. (although neither is forest-dependent), as are the near-threatened Madagascar Pond-heron *Ardeola idae*, Madagascar Crested Ibis *Lophotibis cristata*, Madagascar Cuckoo-falcon *Aviceda madagascariensis* and Madagascar Sparrowhawk *Accipiter madagascariensis* (additional records from Nicoll and Langrand 1986b). Threatened lemurs present are the Woolly Lemur *Avahi laniger* (K), Verreaux's Sifaka *Propithecus verreauxi* (K), Mongoose Lemur *L. mongoz* (V), Milne Edwards's Sportive Lemur *Lepilemur edwardsi* (K); the area is also important for the rodent *Macrotarsomys ingens*; three reptiles, *Brookesia decaryi*, *Pygomeles petteri* and *Chamaeleo angeli*, are known only from the Ankarafantsika Plateau, and two threatened butterflies, *Papilio morondavana* (V) and *P. grosesmithi* (R), occur at the site (Jenkins 1987; also Collins and Morris 1985, Nicoll and Langrand 1986b).

Fire is a serious dry-season hazard, cattle penetrate the reserve, there is much poaching; the present staffing level is insufficient and reserve boundaries need proper demarcation (Andriamampianina and Peyrieras 1972, Jenkins 1987). Studies of the mesite and the vanga are needed to determine their distribution, numbers and ecological requirements within the reserve, and as a guide to where else they should be sought.

62. Andohahela R. N. I. (Parcel 1)   24°45'S 46°45'E
Andohahela is in south-easternmost Madagascar and is divided into three parcels,
parcel 1 with rainforest, parcel 2 with deciduous spiny forest and parcel 3 with
transitional bush/palm forest (O'Connor *et al.* 1985). Of concern here is the
rainforest parcel, difficult of access and ranging from 100 m in the valleys to
1,956 m at its highest point; vegetation is submontane tropical evergreen
rainforest, rich in epiphytes, with canopy height about 25 m though some trees as
high as 35 m; mean annual temperature is around 23°C, mean annual rainfall is
above 2,000 mm (O'Connor *et al.* 1985). The parcel covers 63,100 ha and forms
part of a reserve protected as Réserve Naturelle Intégrale no. 11: Massif
d'Andohahela (Andriamampianina and Peyrieras 1972, O'Connor *et al.* 1985).
   The Scaly Ground-roller *Brachypteracias squamiger* (R) and the near-threatened
Madagascar Crested Ibis *Lophotibis cristata* and Madagascar Sparrowhawk
Accipiter madagascariensis occur in Andohahela parcel 1 (additional records from
O'Connor *et al.* 1985). It is likely that several other threatened bird species, e.g.
Brown Mesite *Mesitornis unicolor* (K) and Pollen's Vanga *Xenopirostris polleni*
(R), will be found in this forest, since the area remains little explored or
documented.   Seven threatened lemurs, including Aye-aye *Daubentonia
madagascariensis* (E), and at least three other threatened mammals occur or are
reported to occur (O'Connor *et al.* 1985).
   Although much of parcel 1 is intact, areas are commonly burnt and clearance
for firewood and cultivation occurs; settlements and livestock encroach within the
boundaries and hunting is a serious problem in the north-east (O'Connor *et al.*
1985). Revision and delineation of reserve boundaries, increased number of
guards, provision of transport for the chief guard, and the promotion of local
development schemes have been called for (O'Connor *et al.* 1985), and the middle
two of these proposals have been implemented (S. M. O'Connor verbally 1987).

63. Tsarafidy (and Ankazomivady) Forests   21°09' 47°10'E
These small patches of forest lie north of Fianarantsoa in south-central
Madagascar, Tsarafidy (= Ankafana, Ankafina) at between 1,300 and 1,500 m
(Griveaud 1961), Ankazomivady (= Nandihizina, Nandihizana) presumably the
same (20°47'S 47°10'E). The relief is hilly, the forest (at Tsarafidy at least)
partially screened as a result; the vegetation is generally that of the eastern humid
rainforest, from which Tsarafidy is (or was in 1961) separated by some 20 km,
Ankazomivady by 12 km or more (Deans Cowan 1882, Griveaud 1961, Tattersall
1986). Dominant trees are *Symphonia* (Guttiferae) and *Cussonia* (Araliaceae), and
epiphytes are abundant; but stature is relatively low, trees only reaching 15 m and
closed canopy descending well below 10 m (Tattersall 1986). Mean annual
rainfall is between 1,200 and 1,500 mm, mean annual temperature around 18°C
(Rand 1936).
   The Grey-crowned Greenbul *Phyllastrephus cinereiceps* (R), Pollen's Vanga
Xenopirostris polleni (R) and Madagascar Yellowbrow *Crossleyia xanthophrys* (I)
occur in Tsarafidy, as do the near-threatened Madagascar Crested Ibis *Lophotibis
cristata* (Griveaud 1961), Pitta-like Ground-roller *Atelornis pittoides* and Brown
Emu-tail   *Dromaeocercus brunneus*;   the   Yellowbrow   is   recorded   from
Ankazomivady (Deans Cowan 1882). Tsarafidy also holds the Diademed Sifaka
Propithecus diadema (V), Ruffed Lemur *Varecia variegata* (I) and Weasel Lemur
Lepilemur mustelinus (K), Ankazomivady held Diademed Sifakas and Ruffed
Lemurs (Deans Cowan 1882); there is no modern confirmation of lemur presence
in either forest (Tattersall 1986). Tsarafidy is the type- (and possibly still the

only) locality for a whole series of insects and also holds an interesting flora including numerous orchids (Griveaud 1961).

Parts of Tsarafidy, especially around the edges, were seriously damaged by wood-cutting (notably for charcoal) by around 1960, but forest on steep inclines remained almost intact; approaches were to be made at that time to increase protection of the forest (Griveaud 1961) but no action appears to have resulted. Ankazomivady is in theory protected as "forêt classé", but is today represented by remnant patches still being cut and burnt (Tattersall 1986). Both forests clearly now require survey.

64. Ranomafana   21°16'S 47°28'E

This is an area of forest in central-south Madagascar, 70 km north-east of Fianarantsoa. The terrain consists of steep-sided hills with some cliffs, intersected with numerous minor tributaries of the sharply falling Namorona river, at an altitude of 800-1,000 m; vegetation is rainforest of the "central Malagasy" type (only the eastern part, away from a bisecting road, is primary), with annual rainfall averaging 2,600 mm (O. Langrand *in litt.* 1987). The total area involved is unknown; the forest is "classé" but the legal protection enjoyed is unknown (O. Langrand *in litt.* 1987).

The Brown Mesite *Mesitornis unicolor* (K), Short-legged Ground-roller *Brachypteracias leptosomus* (R), Rufous-headed Ground-roller *Atelornis crossleyi* (R), Grey-crowned Greenbul *Phyllastrephus cinereiceps* (R), Madagascar Yellowbrow *Crossleyia xanthophrys* (I) and Pollen's Vanga *Xenopirostris polleni* (R) occur in Ranomafana, as do the near-threatened Madagascar Crested Ibis *Lophotibis cristata*, Madagascar Cuckoo-falcon *Aviceda madagascariensis*, Henst's Goshawk *Accipiter henstii*, Pitta-like Ground-roller *Atelornis pittoides*, Wedge-tailed Jery *Hartertula flavoviridis*, Brown Emu-tail *Dromaeocercus brunneus*, Rand's Warbler *Randia pseudozosterops* and Ward's Flycatcher *Pseudobias wardi* (O. Langrand *in litt.* 1987; also Dee 1986). The Greater Bamboo Lemur or Broad-nosed Gentle Lemur *Hapalemur simus* (E), an extremely rare species, has been discovered at Ranomafana (Godfrey and Vuillaume-Randriamanantena 1986, P. Wright *in litt.* to S. M. O'Connor, 1986), although the animals in question are now thought likely to prove a new species (M. E. Nicoll *in litt.* 1987). To date, 23 mammal species, 94 birds and six reptiles have been recorded (O. Langrand *in litt.* 1987).

Clearance and cultivation, even on the steeper slopes, is reducing the forest area, which deserves protected area status to benefit not only the wildlife but also an existing local hydroelectric scheme that utilises the waters of the Namorona (O. Langrand *in litt.* 1987).

65. Périnet-Analamazaotra Faunal Reserve   18°28'S 48°28'E

The Réserve Spéciale d'Analamazaotra lies at 930-1,040 m in mountainous country 150 km east of Antananarivo on the main road to the east coast (Jenkins 1987). Soils are mainly lateritic; the vegetation is high, epiphyte-rich rainforest (characteristic genera being *Weinmannia*, *Tambourissa*, *Symphonia*, *Dalbergia*, *Ravensara* and *Vernonia*), mean annual rainfall 1,721 mm (dry season June-October), mean annual temperature between 20 and 22°C (Rand 1936, Nicoll and Langrand 1986b, Jenkins 1987). The Faunal Reserve covers 8.1 sq km but there are plans to extend it to 100 sq km (Jenkins 1987).

The Madagascar Serpent Eagle *Eutriorchis astur* (E), Brown Mesite *Mesitornis unicolor* (K), Slender-billed Flufftail *Sarothrura watersi* (I), Madagascar Red Owl

Tyto soumagnei (I), Short-legged Ground-roller *Brachypteracias leptosomus* (R), Scaly Ground-roller *B. squamiger* (R), Rufous-headed Ground-roller *Atelornis crossleyi* (R), Yellow-bellied Sunbird-asity *Neodrepanis hypoxantha* (I), Dusky Greenbul *Phyllastrephus tenebrosus* (R), Pollen's Vanga *Xenopirostris polleni* (R) and Madagascar Yellowbrow *Crossleyia xanthophrys* (I) have all been recorded in the Périnet area (although the flufftail is not certainly forest-dependent). The near-threatened Madagascar Pond-heron *Ardeola idae*, Madagascar Crested Ibis *Lophotibis cristata*, Madagascar Cuckoo-falcon *Aviceda madagascariensis*, Henst's Goshawk *Accipiter henstii*, Madagascar Sparrowhawk *A. madagascariensis*, Banded Kestrel *Falco zoniventris*, Pitta-like Ground-roller *Atelornis pittoides*, Bernier's Vanga *Oriolia bernieri*, Wedge-tailed Jery *Hartertula flavoviridis*, Brown Emu-tail *Dromaeocercus brunneus*, Rand's Warbler *Randia pseudozosterops* and Ward's Flycatcher *Pseudobias wardi* are also recorded there. Threatened mammals of the area include Indris *Indri indri* (E), Woolly Lemur *Avahi laniger* (K), Diademed Sifaka *Propithecus diadema* (V), Aye-aye *Daubentonia madagascariensis* (E) and Ruffed Lemur *Varecia variegata* (I) (the reserve has the richest mammalian species assemblage known in Madagascar: M. E. Nicoll *in litt.* 1987); five amphibians, *Paracophyla tuberculata*, *Mantella aurantica*, *Mantidactylus eiselti*, *Boophis reticulatus* and *B. viridis*, and three reptiles, *Lygodactylus guibei*, *Phelsuma flavigularis* and *Brookesia therezieni*, are only known from the Périnet area (Jenkins 1987).

No threat to the reserve is known, although surrounding forest is in less pristine condition (Jenkins 1987). Nevertheless, the proposals to extend the area under protection (see above) make sense since the present dimensions of the reserve seem scarcely likely to guarantee the viability of vertebrate populations in the long term. The records of the Yellow-bellied Sunbird-asity – the only observations up to 1986 since the species was described – were from a few kilometres above the reserve and it is to be hoped that the new boundaries will incorporate this higher area. Périnet-Analamazaotra has a very high score of 44 and ranks 4th among the forests considered in this review (2nd on Madagascar).

66. "Sihanaka Forest"   18°00'S 48°45'E

"Sihanaka Forest" is the name (technically incorrect, as the Sihanaka people do not live there) apparently imposed by explorers to stand crudely for the broad belt of humid forest that lies between the east coast and the Mangoro valley, east and south of Lake Alaotra and in particular in the Tamatave hinterland between the towns of Didy and Fito (see Collar and Stuart 1985:154). The statement by Stresemann (1926) that Sihanaka is the "large forest west of Fénérive" (i.e. well to the north of the area defined here) is so out of conformity with other evidence that it must be considered erroneous. South of Didy and Fito the forest belt appears to narrow and fragment (Périnet – see above – is one of the preserved pieces) in the face of heavy human settlement between the capital and the coast; to the north the belt broadens into the area of unexplored forest which may yet prove the most important in Madagascar referred to in the note introducing this section. The limits – wholly artificial – used for definition here are roughly the Didy-Fito area north to the Zahamena R.N.I. The region thus defined is rugged, mid-altitude (500-1,300 m) terrain with steep-sided valleys, holding primary and secondary evergreen rainforest changing (in Zahamena at least) from that characterised by Myristicaceae and *Anthostema* at low altitude to that with *Tambourissa* and *Weinmannia* above 800 m; annual rainfall is between 1,500 and 2,000 mm (higher towards the east) and annual temperature between 20 and 22°C

(Andriamampianina and Peyrieras 1972; also Rand 1936). The area of Zahamena R.N.I. (Strict Nature Reserve) is 732 sq km (Andriamampianina and Peyrieras 1972) but the total area of "Sihanaka Forest" as defined above is several times this size, none of this additional surface being protected.

The Madagascar Serpent Eagle *Eutriorchis astur* (E), Brown Mesite *Mesitornis unicolor* (K), Madagascar Red Owl *Tyto soumagnei* (I), Short-legged Ground-roller *Brachypteracias leptosomus* (R), Scaly Ground-roller *B. squamiger* (R), Rufous-headed Ground-roller *Atelornis crossleyi* (R), Yellow-bellied Sunbird-asity *Neodrepanis hypoxantha* (I), Dusky Greenbul *Phyllastrephus tenebrosus* (R), Grey-crowned Greenbul *P. cinereiceps* (R), Pollen's Vanga *Xenopirostris polleni* (R) and Madagascar Yellowbrow *Crossleyia xanthophrys* (I) have all been recorded from Sihanaka Forest. The near-threatened Madagascar Crested Ibis *Lophotibis cristata*, Madagascar Cuckoo-falcon *Aviceda madagascariensis*, Henst's Goshawk *Accipiter henstii*, Madagascar Sparrowhawk *A. madagascariensis*, Banded Kestrel *Falco zoniventris*, Pitta-like Ground-roller *Atelornis pittoides*, Bernier's Vanga *Oriolia bernieri*, Wedge-tailed Jery *Hartertula flavoviridis*, Brown Emu-tail *Dromaeocercus brunneus* and Ward's Flycatcher *Pseudobias wardi* are also recorded there. Threatened mammals of the region include Indris *Indri indri* (E), Woolly Lemur *Avahi laniger* (K), Diademed Sifaka *Propithecus diadema* (V), Ruffed Lemur *Varecia variegata* (I) and Grey Gentle Lemur *Hapalemur griseus* (K) (Jenkins 1987).

The extent of forest clearance in the region is unknown, but a report that Sihanaka's "original evergreen forest has been completely eliminated" (Benson and Irwin 1972) was mistaken (D. A. Turner and A. D. Forbes-Watson verbally 1984). In Zahamena R.N.I. there are villages which present a growing threat; cultivation, livestock grazing and poaching occur within its boundaries (Andriamampianina and Peyrieras 1972). Survey-work of Zahamena took place in 1985, and the protection of Sihanaka has been urgent, since it is, on present knowledge, the single most important area of unprotected bird habitat in Madagascar. Sihanaka Forest has a very high score of 46 and ranks 3rd among the forests considered in this review (1st on Madagascar).

67. Tsaratanana Massif   14°00'S 49°00'E

The Massif du Tsaratanana lies in the far north-west of Madagascar. It consists of crystalline rocks and acid volcanic formations, very rugged and mountainous, its highest peak (Mont Maromokotro, 2,876 m) being the highest in the island; while the massif represents the northernmost extension of the island's central chain of mountains, the forest that swathes it represents an extension north-west of the eastern rainforest belt, and comprises primary and secondary growth from low to high altitude, with many endemic plant species and abundant epiphytes (Andriamampianina and Peyrieras 1972). Annual rainfall is 2,000-3,000 mm, with a short season of relatively dry weather in October and November (Rand 1936). The area of the massif under forest is unknown, but the main part of it is under protection as the Réserve Naturelle Intégrale (Strict Nature Reserve) de Tsaratanana, which covers 486 sq km, though not all of this is forested (Andriamampianina and Peyrieras 1972).

The Rufous-headed Ground-roller *Atelornis crossleyi* (R), Grey-crowned Greenbul *Phyllastrephus cinereiceps* (R) and Madagascar Yellowbrow *Crossleyia xanthophrys* (I) occur in Tsaratanana, as do the near-threatened Wedge-tailed Jery *Hartertula flavoviridis*, Brown Emu-tail *Dromaeocercus brunneus* and Ward's Flycatcher *Pseudobias wardi*. Threatened mammals of the region include the

Fork-marked Lemur *Phaner furcifer* (K), Black Lemur *Lemur macaco* (E/V), Red-bellied Lemur *L. rubriventer* (I) and Grey Gentle Lemur *Hapalemur griseus* (K); three amphibians, *Mantipus guentherpetersi*, *Platyhyla alticola* and *Platypelis tsaratananaensis*, two reptiles, *Chamaeleo tsaratananensis* and *Amphiglossus tsaratananensis*, and no fewer than 30 molluscs are known only from the massif (Jenkins 1987).

The extent of forest clearance in the region is unknown. In Tsaratanana R.N.I. the forest is largely intact and the terrain provides some natural protection, but vigilance is needed to prevent the establishment of illegal plantations such as were discovered in the late 1960s (Andriamampianina and Peyrieras 1972). The major requirement for birds is further survey, since the area is virtually unexplored.

68. Forests around Maroantsetra   15°23'S 49°44'E

The forests in question (or what remains of them) are that part of the eastern rainforest belt of Madagascar that lies in the lowlands, foothills and mountains that ring Maroantsetra at the top and along the western side of Antongil Bay, i.e. from sea-level up to c.1,000 m.   The evergreen rainforest is tall with closed canopy and many epiphytes, but with relatively sparse ground-cover in lower areas; annual rainfall in the area is the highest in Madagascar, over 3,500 mm with little seasonal variation, the mean annual temperature ranges from 23.6°C on the coast to 20°C a little way inland, and humidity is high (Rand 1936). None of the forest in the region is protected.

The Madagascar Serpent Eagle *Eutriorchis astur* (E), Brown Mesite *Mesitornis unicolor* (K), Short-legged Ground-roller *Brachypteracias leptosomus* (R), Scaly Ground-roller *B. squamiger* (R) and Pollen's Vanga *Xenopirostris polleni* (R) are recorded from these forests, as are the near-threatened Madagascar Crested Ibis *Lophotibis cristata*, Madagascar Cuckoo-falcon *Aviceda madagascariensis*, Réunion Harrier *Circus maillardi*, Henst's Goshawk *Accipiter henstii*, Madagascar Sparrowhawk *A. madagascariensis*, Banded Kestrel *Falco zoniventris*, Pitta-like Ground-roller *Atelornis pittoides*, Bernier's Vanga *Oriolia bernieri*, Rand's Warbler *Randia pseudozosterops* and Ward's Flycatcher *Pseudobias wardi* (see Dee 1986). Threatened mammals of the region include Indris *Indri indri* (E), Woolly Lemur *Avahi laniger* (K), Diademed Sifaka *Propithecus diadema* (V), Aye-aye *Daubentonia madagascariensis* (E), Hairy-eared Dwarf Lemur *Allocebus trichotis* (E), Red-bellied Lemur *Lemur rubriventer* (I), Ruffed Lemur *Varecia variegata* (I), Broad-nosed Gentle Lemur *Hapalemur simus* (E), Grey Gentle Lemur *H. griseus* (K), and Weasel Lemur *Lepilemur mustelinus* (K) (Jenkins 1987); the bat *Myzopoda aurita*, the sole member of its family, has in recent years only been seen in the Maroantsetra region (M. E. Nicoll *in litt.* 1987), and at least one reptile, *Typhlops ocularis*, and three molluscs, *Boucardicus nanus*, *Cyclotus millotti* and *Omphalotropis arbusculae*, are known only from Maroantsetra's forests (Jenkins 1987).

Forest in the Maroantsetra region has suffered considerably from clearance (Keith *et al.* 1974).   Biological research there has been almost totally lacking yet, because of the particularly high rainfall, certain features unique to the region might be expected.   This is therefore an important area for primary research and exploration.   A call for strict protection of Madagascar's remaining primary forests used those around Maroantsetra as the example (Resolution 7, recommendation 1, in IUCN 1972). Very recently, 75,000 ha of lowlands (including 23,000 ha of reserved forest) at Mananara Nord have been proposed as

a Biosphere Reserve (Nicoll and Langrand 1986b). Maroantsetra has a high score
of 25 and ranks 18th= among the forests considered in this review.

69. Marojejy R.N.I. and Andapa region   14°26'S 49°15'E

The Réserve Naturelle Intégrale de Marojejy lies north-west of Andapa in
Diégo-Suarez province; the area one day's march west of Andapa has also been
found to be important (see Rand 1936) and for present purposes this and the
reserve are considered as one locality. Marojejy comprises a very rugged gneissic
massif rising to 2,137 m, with a succession of vegetation-types: at 50-800 m there
is a high "ombrophilous" forest, dense, humid and evergreen, with a canopy often
higher than 30 m and with emergent *Canarium madagascariensis* and *Sloanea
rhodantha* up to 40-45 m; at 800-1,450 m a montane ombrophilous forest, dense,
humid, epiphyte-rich ("moss-forest"), with the canopy down to 20 m and a
herbaceous understorey rich in spectacularly coloured flowers; at 1,450-1,850 m
dense sclerophyllous lichen forest, thereafter a scrubby ericaceous vegetation
(Andriamampianina and Peyrieras 1972, Guillaumet *et al.* 1975); one day west of
Andapa at around 1,800 m moss- and lichen-forest occurred along with stands of
taller forest more characteristic of lowlands (Rand 1936).   Annual rainfall is
claimed to be the highest in Madagascar at over 3,000 mm, this being on the east
and south-east sides above 1,400-1,500 m (Andriamampianina and Peyrieras 1972,
Guillaumet *et al.* 1975) but the data mapped in Rand (1936), while confirming the
figure, indicate that the Antongil Bay region is rainier (see entry on forests
around Maroantsetra above); annual rainfall at Andapa is 2,042 mm (Guillaumet
et al. 1975). Maximum cloud is at c.1,800 m, with the summits often dry and
exposed to periods of strong insolation (Guillaumet *et al.* 1975). Temperatures
show a wide range with altitude, but the annual mean appears (from data mapped
in Rand 1936) nowhere to exceed 20°C; the range at Andapa is 13.5-19.5°C
(Guillaumet *et al.* 1975).   The area of the R.N.I. (Strict Nature Reserve) is
601 sq km (Andriamampianina and Peyrieras 1972).

The Slender-billed Flufftail *Sarothrura watersi* (I), Short-legged Ground-roller
Brachypteracias leptosomus (R), Scaly Ground-roller *B. squamiger* (R),
Rufous-headed Ground-roller *Atelornis crossleyi* (R), possibly also the Madagascar
Serpent Eagle *Eutriorchis astur* (E) and Pollen's Vanga *Xenopirostris polleni* (R),
occur in Marojejy and west of Andapa (though the flufftail is not certainly
forest-dependent).   The near-threatened Madagascar Crested Ibis *Lophotibis
cristata*, Madagascar Cuckoo-falcon *Aviceda madagascariensis*, Réunion Harrier
Circus maillardi, Henst's Goshawk *Accipiter henstii*, Madagascar Sparrowhawk *A.
madagascariensis*, Banded Kestrel *Falco zoniventris*, Pitta-like Ground-roller
Atelornis pittoides, Bernier's Vanga *Oriolia bernieri*, Rand's Warbler *Randia
pseudozosterops* and Ward's Flycatcher *Pseudobias wardi* are also recorded there
(additional information from Nicoll and Langrand 1986b).   Threatened mammals
of the region include Diademed Sifaka *Propithecus diadema* (V) and Grey Gentle
Lemur *Hapalemur griseus* (K); seven amphibians, *Mantipus minutus*, *M.
serratopalpebrosus*, *Stumpffia grandis*, *S. roseifemoralis*, *S. tridactyla*,
Mantidactylus klemmeri and *M. pseudoasper*, and two reptiles, *Brookesia karchei*
and *B. griveaudi*, are known only from Marojejy, as are two molluscs, *Ampelita
globulus* and *Malagrion paenelimax* (Jenkins 1987).   There are several endemic
palms, ferns and orchids, with some 2,000 plants in total in the reserve (Jenkins
1987).   Marojejy is considered the most impressive massif in Madagascar, on
account of its scenic grandeur, floristic richness and, above all, undisturbed
condition (Andriamampianina and Peyrieras 1972).

Some check needs to be exerted on continuing intrusion into the reserve by shifting cultivators at lower levels (Andriamampianina and Peyrieras 1972, M. E. Nicoll *in litt.* 1987). An intensive study of the area's avifauna is most important. Marojejy and Andapa have a high score of 26 and rank 16th= among the forests considered in this review.

Notes added in proof In August and September 1988 the Cambridge Madagascar Rainforest Expedition surveyed Marojejy R.N.I. for birds and other animals and, among other things, confirmed the presence there (as well as the global survival) of the Madagascar Serpent Eagle, and also found Brown Mesite *Mesitornis unicolor* (K), Madagascar Yellowbrow *Crossleyia xanthophrys* (I) and Grey-crownéd Greenbul *Phyllastrephus cinereiceps* (R) (B. Sheldon, R. Wilkinson verbally 1988; details will be published in an ICBP Study Report).

In 1987 a survey of Ankarana cliffs and Analamera area in northern Madagascar confirmed the presence there of the Madagascar Fish-eagle *Haliaeetus vociferoides* (E), White-breasted Mesite *Mesitornis variegata* (R) and Van Dam's Vanga *Xenopirostris damii* (R), along with several other important animals, most notably Aye-aye *Daubentonia madagascariensis* (E) and Diademed Sifaka *Propithecus diadema* (V) in the highly threatened and endemic race *perrieri* (A. Hawkins, P. Chapman verbally 1988). This area thus takes its place as a site of real importance for conservation in Madagascar although, as noted in the introduction to this section, many more areas of sympatric occurrence of threatened species can be expected to come to light in future years.

ISLANDS

The most critically threatened birds in the Afrotropical and Malagasy Realm occur on oceanic islands, and many of these are forest species. Extinctions of birds have been documented on a number of these islands, notably Mauritius, compared with none so far on the African mainland. In this review we identify six forests (Map 1a,b; also Maps 3 and 6) of particular importance for forest bird conservation on islands around Africa:

No.	Forest area	Priority score	Position among all the forests in this review
75	Macchabé/Bel Ombre Nature Reserve, Mauritius	64	1
70	Forests in south-west São Tomé	56	2
72	Mount Karthala, Comoro Islands	25	19=
73	Mahé Highlands, Seychelles	17	26
74	Plaine des Chicots, Réunion (France)	8	50=
71	Mount Malabo, Equatorial Guinea	7	55

Details of the priority scores and how they are calculated are given in the introductory section "Priorities for Conservation Action". These forest island avifaunas are important because they are very distinct from each other, as well as being highly threatened. The threats to these avifaunas often have as much to do with ecological problems caused by introduced species as they do with forest clearance.

70. Forests in south-west São Tomé (São Tomé e Príncipe) 0°08'N 6°30'E

The island of São Tomé, situated in the Gulf of Guinea almost on the equator, rises to 2,024 m, and the high ground around and to the south of the main peak is swathed in forest: the area of most luxuriant growth appears to have produced the most important bird records and is perhaps most simply defined as the area demarcated by the 4,000 mm isohyet (i.e. from the main peak west to the west coast and south-east to the coast at São João dos Angolares). São Tomé is mountainous and of volcanic origin; in the west-central and southern sections there are at least 10 impressive peaks above 1,000 m, the highest of these being Cabumbé (1,403 m), where the Rio Quija has its source (MC 1948, Abshire and Samuels 1969, Bredero *et al.* 1977, Günther and Feiler 1985). The soils of the south-west are humic and ferralitic, in the southern part with litholic soils and lithosols (Lains e Silva 1958); although most lowland rainforest has been cleared for plantations, there is such forest (below 800 m) in the south-west, while from 800 to 1,400 m there is "mountain-forest" (Exell 1944, Monod 1960, Bredero *et al.* 1977). This latter consists of tall straight trees usually branching at a great height to form a dense canopy, with festoons of lianas, trunks swathed in epiphytes, and an undergrowth of small bushes, orchids and ferns; indeed the main features of this forest type are (1) the relatively large number of species in a very small area, (2) the preponderance of madders Rubiaceae and spurges Euphorbiaceae, (3) the absence or paucity of legumes Leguminosae and composites Compositae, (4) the great development of epiphytes, notably the orchids Orchidaceae, and (5) the profusion of ferns Filicinae, which possibly reach their greatest abundance and diversity anywhere in Africa (Exell 1944). Rainfall in the south-west, as noted above, is exceptionally high, and nowhere in the area is the annual mean below 4,000 mm, but a less wet season occurs in July and August; mean annual temperatures for the altitudes 0-800 m and 800-1,400 m lie between 18 and 26°C and 13 and 18°C respectively (Bredero et al. 1977). The area of forest in south-west São Tomé is unknown but cannot be at all large (and certainly less than 200 sq km); none of it is known to be officially protected, although logging licences are required to cut it and these are not granted (Jones and Tye 1988).

The Dwarf Olive Ibis Bostrychia bocagei (I), Maroon Pigeon Columba thomensis (V), São Tomé Scops Owl Otus hartlaubi (R), São Tomé Fiscal Shrike Lanius newtoni (I), São Tomé Short-tail Amaurocichla bocagii (I), São Tomé White-eye Zosterops ficedulinus (I) and São Tomé Grosbeak Neospiza concolor (I), as well as the São Tomé Thrush Turdus olivaceofuscus (n-t), São Tomé Paradise Flycatcher Terpsiphone atrochalybea (n-t) and Giant Sunbird Dreptes thomensis (n-t), i.e. all the threatened and near-threatened birds of São Tomé (of which only the White-eye, perhaps the Owl, and possibly still the Thrush – which at least used to occur on Príncipe – are not wholly endemic to the island) occur or have occurred in the forests of the south-west. In addition, five other single island endemic species (counting the Speirops) occur in these forests as well as five (not counting Otus) others shared only with Príncipe (Jones and Tye 1988). Two mammals, the São Tomé Little Collared Fruit-bat Myonycteris brachycephala and the São Tomé White-toothed Shrew Crocidura thomensis, are endemic to the island, as are three amphibians, the two tree frogs Hyperolius molleri and H. thomensis and the caecilian Schistometopum ephele, while two further caecilians, two geckoes, two burrowing snakes and a skink only otherwise occur on Príncipe (Jones and Tye 1988; B. Groombridge in litt. 1987 to P. J. Jones and T. H. Johnson). Of at least 601 indigenous plants recorded in the 1930s 108 are endemic (Exell 1944, 1973): it is likely that a high proportion of these endemics are present in – and a lesser but still significant proportion confined to – forests of the south-west.

Much of the forest cover in south-west São Tomé is probably permanently protected by the rugged terrain on which it grows, but it is possible that the lack of records for certain birds in the past 50 years is attributable to loss of particular areas of lowland forest, much of which took place during the conversion of the island's economy to cocoa-production, 1890-1910 (de Campos 1956): Exell (1952) refers to there now being "nowhere an unbroken altitudinal succession", but Lains e Silva (1958) maps primary forest descending almost to the coast in south-west São Tomé, with only a thin belt of intervening second growth. Appropriate conservation measures for São Tomé's forests cannot be propounded without a complete reassessment of the island's habitats and wildlife, now in progress (Jones and Tye 1988). The forests in south-west São Tomé have an extremely high score, ranking 2nd among all the forests considered in this review.

71. Mount Malabo, Bioko (Equatorial Guinea) 3°36'N 8°45'E
The main peak on Bioko (formerly Fernando Po), Mount Malabo (formerly Pico de Santa Isabel or Pico Basilé), dominates the northern half of the island. It is volcanic in origin (like Bioko itself) and supports (though now much destroyed) lowland rainforest up to 900 m, montane forest up to 2,400 m, and montane heathland thence to the peak at 3,008 m (Eisentraut 1973), although from 1,900 m to the treeline "lichen forest" predominates. Annual rainfall in montane parts of Bioko varies from 2,500 to 4,000 mm, temperature (on Mount Malabo at 2,000 m) varies from 12.8°C at night to 24.6°C by day, though in the alpine summit zone it drops occasionally as low as 0°C (Eisentraut 1973). The area of forest on Mount Malabo is several hundred sq km (T. M. Butynski *in litt.* 1987) (although that specifically occupied by the Fernando Po Speirops *Speirops brunneus* will be somewhat less than this, the species being confined to lichen forest and the heath zone); none of it appears to be officially protected although natural vegetation on the island above 800 m has been little affected by human activities (T. M. Butynski verbally 1986).

The Fernando Po Speirops (R) is confined to the upper forest on Mount Malabo, and the Cameroon Mountain Roughwing *Psalidoprocne fuliginosa* (n-t) is recorded there. In addition, the Grey-necked Picathartes *Picathartes oreas* (R) has recently been discovered in the south-west of Bioko (T. M. Butynski verbally 1986). The Fernando Po Swift *Apus sladeniae* (K) is known from the island, although this is unlikely to be a forest species, and Ursula's Mouse-coloured Sunbird *Nectarinia ursulae* (n-t) is also present in forest at intermediate elevations on the island. Preuss's Guenon *Cercopithecus preussi* (V) occurs on Mount Malabo (T. M. Butynski verbally 1986). It should be pointed out that the south-western corner of the island, where 350 sq km of forest survives, is also important for conservation and some rare primates survive in these forests, including the Drill *Papio leucophaeus* (E), Russet-eared Guenon *Cercopithecus erythrotis* (V) and the Black Colobus *Colobus satanus* (E) (Oates 1986, T. M. Butynski verbally 1986). A skink *Scelotes poensis* and a caecilian *Schistometopum garzonheydti* are endemic to the island (B. Groombridge *in litt.* to T. H. Johnson, 1987), and presumably occur in the forested regions.

Although there appears to be little official protection of the forests on Mount Malabo, the conservation situation here, as elsewhere on Bioko, is remarkably good. This is because no rainforest clearance has taken place in the past 10-20 years, one-third of the agricultural land has been abandoned owing to the collapse of the cocoa industry, and the government confiscated guns in the hands of the civilian population in 1974 (T. M. Butynski verbally 1986). There is now an urgent need to incorporate protected areas and conservation policies as part of the country's economic reconstruction, perhaps as part of a National Conservation Strategy. The area above 800 m on Mount Malabo merits protection (Castroviejo *et al.* 1986).

72. Mount Karthala on Grand Comoro (Comoro Islands) 11°50'S 43°20'E
This is the main peak of Grand Comoro, in the southern half of the island. It is an active volcano, rising to 2,361 m, dome-shaped and fairly steeply sloping; the entire island has only a very thin topsoil and consists mainly of recent lava without permanent watercourses, rain simply draining into the volcanic rock (Louette *et al.* 1986). On the western and south-eastern slopes of Mount Karthala evergreen rainforest exists in areas that were over 94 and 17 sq km respectively in the 1940s (while on other slopes more open, recent forest stands on bare lava-

slag); in the 1950s the forest on the western slope extended as far as 1,900 m
and as low as 550 m (Benson 1960), and this situation still generally obtains,
though most forest elsewhere on the mountain lies between 800 and 1,400 m and
parts have suffered degradation in recent decades, the best areas being the humid
south-west and drier, inaccessible east flanks (Louette et al. 1986). Rainfall
reaches over 5,600 mm per year on the west flank of Mount Karthala, which is
exposed to the north-west monsoon (the hottest and most humid season) from
November to April, trade winds from May to October generally bringing cooler,
drier weather; mean annual temperature at 1,000 m would be around 19°C
(Louette et al. 1986). None of the forest on Mount Karthala is protected.

The Grand Comoro Scops Owl Otus pauliani (R), Grand Comoro Flycatcher
Humblotia flavirostris (R), Mount Karthala White-eye Zosterops mouroniensis (R)
and Grand Comoro Drongo Dicrurus fuscipennis (R) are all restricted to Mount
Karthala. That the near-threatened Mrs Benson's Warbler Nesillas mariae,
otherwise confined to Moheli, has been recorded from its lower slopes, as
reported in Collar and Stuart (1985), is now understood to be an error (M.
Louette in litt. 1987).

Clearance of the lower forest for agriculture now occurs on an apparently
serious scale, timber exploitation is proceeding at an unknown pace, and a hiking
track that was being constructed in 1983-1984 to the crater rim carries the risk of
being upgraded to a road, which might then increase the chances of further
habitat destruction and tourist disturbance (Louette et al. 1986). Protected area
status for a representative section of Mount Karthala is required, and an area has
been delineated for possible national park gazetting (in Louette et al. 1986).
Mount Karthala has a high score of 25 and ranks 18th= among the forests considered in this review.

73. Central highland rainforest, Mahé (Seychelles)   4°40'S 55°30'E
This forest extends from around Le Niol Peak (Mount Simpson) in west Mahé
along the central ridge south-east to Cascade estate in the east-central section of
the island. The relief is rugged and steep, the underlying rock granite, the highest
point 905 m (see Braithwaite 1984, Walsh 1984). The forest important for birds
lies between 250 and 600 m, in ravines and in slopes and valley-sides; it is much
invaded by exotic vegetation (principal components of native and endemic flora
are given in Vesey-FitzGerald 1940; see also Procter 1984). Mean annual rainfall
(not adequately recorded) appears to lie above 3,000 mm (3,250 mm at Salazie,
407 m), most rain (at lower altitudes at least) falling between October and March
(summer period); mean annual temperature at La Misère (580 m) is probably
around 23°C with little annual range (Walsh 1984). Most of the area in question
– from Le Niol Peak south-east as far as La Misère and Souvenir – falls within
the Morne Seychellois National Park, which covers 3,045 ha (although some of
the park includes coastal lowlands) (MOD [DOS] 1978; IUCN/UNEP 1987).

The Seychelles Scops Owl Otus insularis (R), Seychelles Swiftlet Collocalia
elaphra (R) and Seychelles White-eye Zosterops modestus (E) all occur within the
central highland rainforest, although the Swiftlet is not rainforest-dependent and
the other two occur more in forest dominated by exotic species (R. Wilson in litt.
1987); the Seychelles Kestrel Falco araea (O) also occurs there. The Owl and
the White-eye are endemic to Mahé. The Seychelles Sheath-tailed Bat Coleura
seychellensis was once common (nominate race seychellensis) on Mahé but may
now be extinct there (Racey and Nicoll 1984). Most Seychelles reptiles are
present as are at least 10 of the 12 endemic species of amphibian including the

very rare *Praslinia cooperi* (Nussbaum 1984, IUCN/UNEP 1987). The endangered tree *Vateria seychellarum* and many endemic plants grow in this forest (IUCN/UNEP 1987).
Outside the area of the national park, new extraction techniques now permit exploitation of the hitherto inaccessible patches of tall woodland in the remoter valley heads (Wilson 1981). Within the park (a multi-use management area: R. Wilson *in litt.* 1987), some felling has occurred, army exercises are carried out, and exotic species of tree continue to encroach on a large scale (IUCN/UNEP 1987). The identification of stands of vegetation crucial for all endemic fauna and flora would give valuable support to management policy within and even outside the national park.

74. Plaine des Chicots, Réunion (France)   20°58'S 55°28'E
This locality and the much smaller Plaine d'Affouches are adjacent and form a unit of forest inland from St. Denis in north-west Réunion. The "plains" are in fact volcanic slopes bounded by deep gorges covering an altitudinal range (under forest) of some 800 to 1,800 m, and hold three types of vegetation, (a) mixed evergreen forest ("bois de couleurs"), the climax vegetation, (b) tamarin *Acacia heterophylla* forest, a fire-climax related to vulcanism, and (c) *Philippia abietina* heath (Cheke 1987a). Rainfall can often be prodigious during cyclones; temperatures down to -5°C are frequent in the upper part of Plaine des Chicots (Cheke 1987a). The total area involved is 16 sq km and the forest exists as a hunting reserve.
The Réunion Cuckoo-shrike *Coracina newtoni* (V) is restricted to Plaine des Chicots and Plaine d'Affouches.
˘ The forest is at risk from the introduced deer *Cervus timorensis* maintained there at artificially high densities for the purpose of hunting: no regeneration is occurring. A programme of native forest clearance has destroyed such vegetation on Plaine des Chicots up to the 1,200 m contour. A strict nature reserve with proper control of deer is required for the entire remaining area of native forest at this site and Plaine d'Affouches: Cheke (1977) and Bosser (1982) have made detailed recommendations, though the latter's covers an insufficient area to guarantee the safety of the Cuckoo-shrike (A. S. Cheke *in litt.* 1987).

75. Macchabé/Bel Ombre Nature Reserve (Mauritius)   20°25' 55°27'E
This area covers the upper part of the Black River (Grande) Gorge and adjacent plateau areas to the north and south in south-west Mauritius. The plateau areas are at around 600 m (highest point is Black River Peak, 828 m), but the upper part of the Black River Gorge is a steep U-shaped scarp facing west, and there is also a steep south-facing scarp in the south at Bel Ombre; the whole formation is volcanic, soils being highly laterised and immature (Fox *et al.* 1985, Cheke 1987b; see Map 1 in Procter and Salm 1974). Three types of forest are present within the reserve: (1) indigenous wet upland forest at Macchabé (Macabé) and formerly in the Black River Gorge, dominated by trees in the Sapotaceae *Mimusops, Labourdonnaisia, Sideroxylon* spp.), with *Diospyros tesselaria, Erythrospermum monticolum, Gaertnera psychotrioides, Syzygium glomeratum, Securinega durissima, Aphloia theiformis, Tabernaemontana mauritiana* and *Nuxia verticillata*, canopy height 18-21(-25) m with many mosses, lichens and ferns, mean annual rainfall lying between 2,000 and 3,000 mm, annual temperature range from 14 to 26°C (Fox *et al.* 1985, A. S. Cheke *in litt.* 1987); (2) indigenous dwarf forest of the plateau at Plaine Champagne, characterised as

Sideroxylon–Helichrysum "scrub", canopy height being only 3-5 m, with many mosses, lichens and ferns, mean annual rainfall 2,500 mm, annual temperature range from 17 to 22°C (Fox *et al.* 1985, Cheke 1987b); and (3) southern scarp forest at Bel Ombre, dominated in the upper part by *Calophyllum tacamaha* but with the more mixed indigenous upland forest recurring on the lower slopes to 300 m (Cheke 1987b), for which no climatic data are available. The area of the Macchabé/Bel Ombre Nature Reserve is 36 sq km (Collar and Stuart 1985) but the area under native forest is considerably smaller than this, the large areas in the Gorge itself being almost completely degraded and covered with exotic vegetation (A. S. Cheke *in litt.* 1987).

Every threatened (and indeed every endemic) bird on Mauritius occurs within the Macchabé/Bel Ombre Nature Reserve, namely Mauritius Kestrel *Falco punctatus* (E), Pink Pigeon *Nesoenas mayeri* (E), Mauritius Parakeet *Psittacula eques* (E), Mauritius Cuckoo-shrike *Coracina typica* (V), Mauritius Black Bulbul *Hypsipetes olivaceus* (V), Mauritius Olive White-eye *Zosterops chloronothus* (V) and Mauritius Fody *Foudia rubra* (E) (but see below). The Mauritius Flying Fox *Pteropus niger* (R) occurs in Macchabé/Bel Ombre and adjacent forests; the very rare lizard *Scelotes bojerii*, which otherwise survives only on Mauritius's offshore islets, is present in small numbers in Macchabé (Cheke 1987d, A. S. Cheke verbally 1987). The forests of south-west Mauritius hold or held several endemic butterflies and a strong complement of endemic herbivorous snails, though these latter appear to be mostly extinct (A. S. Cheke verbally 1987). The reserve also holds a remarkable number of critically threatened plant species, plant endemism being of a very high order in the Mascarenes and especially Mauritius (Strahm in prep.).

Preservation of the integrity of this reserve is essential to the survival of all the threatened wildlife it contains. However, a matrix of factors contributes to the steady degeneration of the native forest within it and elsewhere in south-west Mauritius: invasion of exotic plants, the seeds of which are further dispersed by various exotic and endemic animals, browsing by introduced deer, grubbing by feral pigs, seed-destruction by introduced monkeys and rats, plus the devastation of cyclones (Collar and Stuart 1985, Cheke 1987c). Work to identify means of minimising and even reversing this degeneration is beginning under the auspices of the Mauritius Wildlife Research and Conservation Programme (P. D. Goriup verbally 1984-1985, also Cheke 1987d), but old proposals to create a national park by combining Macchabé/Bel Ombre Nature Reserve with adjacent forests of the lower Black River Gorges (Procter and Salm 1974) and the southern scarp forests from Mount Cocotte to Mount Savane (see Cheke 1987b), and indeed the elevation of the whole area to World Heritage Site status, merit reconsideration, especially as the main area utilised by the Pink Pigeon, and about half the area occupied by the Black Bulbul, Olive White-eye and Fody, remain outside the existing nature reserve (A. S. Cheke *in litt.* 1987). Macchabé/Bel Ombre has an extremely high score of 64, ranking 1st among all the 75 forests considered in this review.

REFERENCES

Abshire, D. M. and Samuels, M. A., eds. (1969) *Portuguese Africa.* London: Pall Mall.

Adam, J. G. (1966) La végétation du Mont Nimba au Libéria et sa protection. *Notes Africaines* 112: 113-122.

Adam, J. G. (1970) Etat actuel de la végétation des Monts Nimba au Libéria et en Guinée. *Adansonia* 2,10: 193-211.

Adam, J. G. (1971) Flore descriptive des Monts Nimba. *Mém. Mus. Natn. Hist. Nat.* Ser.B. 20: 5-528.

Airy Shaw, H. K. (1947) The vegetation of Angola. *J. Ecol.* 35: 23-48.

Anderson, J. R., Williamson, E. A. and Carter, J. (1983) Chimpanzees of Sapo Forest, Liberia: density, nests, tools and meat-eating. *Primates* 24: 594-601.

Andrews, P., Groves, C. P. and Horne, J. F. M. (1975) Ecology of the Lower Tana River flood plain (Kenya). *J. East Afr. Nat. Hist. Soc. and Natn. Mus.* no. 151.

Andriamampianina, J. and Peyrieras, A. (1972) Les réserves naturelles intégrales de Madagascar. Pp. 103-123 (Communication 10) in *C. R. Conférence Internationale sur la Conservation de la Nature et de ses Ressources à Madagascar.* Morges: IUCN(NS) Doc. suppl. no. 36.

Appert, O. (1968a) Zur Brutbiologie der Erdracke *Uratelornis chimaera* Rothschild. *J. Orn.* 109: 264-275.

Appert, O. (1968b) Beobachtungen an *Monias benschi* in Südwest-Madagascar. *J. Orn.* 109: 402-417.

Appert, O. (1985) Zur Biologie der Mesitornithiformes (Nakas oder "Stelzenrallen") Madagaskars und erste fotografische Dokumente von Vertretern der Ordnung. *Orn. Beob.* 82: 31-54.

Ash, J. S. and Miskell, J. E. (1981) Present abundance of the Warsangli Linnet *Acanthis johannis. Bull. Brit. Orn. Club* 101: 396-398.

Ash, J. S. and Sharland, R. E. (1986) *Nigeria: assessment of bird conservation priorities.* Cambridge, U.K.: International Council for Bird Preservation (Study Report no. 11).

Baker, R. G. E. (1986) Introduction. Pp. 1-13 in R. G. E. Baker, K. Richards and C. A. Rimes, eds. *The Hull University Cameroon Expedition 1981-1982 Final Report.* Hull: University of Hull Department of Geography, Misc. Ser. no. 30.

Banks, P. F. (1976) Editorial: Chirinda Forest. *Rhodesia Science News* 10: 39.

Barbosa, L. A. G. (1970) *Carta fitogeográfica de Angola.* Luanda: Instituto de Investigação Científica de Angola.

Beentje, H. J., Ndiang'ui, N. and Mutangah, J. (1987) Forest islands in the mist. *Swara* 10: 20-21.

Beentje, H. J. and Ndiang'ui, N. (in prep.) Botany of the Taita Hills forests.

Belcher, C. F. (1925) Birds on the Luchenya Plateau, Mlanje, Nyasaland. *Ibis* (12) 1: 797-814.

Bennun, L. (1986)   Montane birds of the Bwindi (Impenetrable) Forest. *Scopus* 10: 87-91.
Bennun, L. (1987)   Ornithological report. Pp. 5-35 in Report of the Cambridge Bwindi Forest Study Group, August-October 1984. Unpublished.
Benson, C. W. (1950)   A collection from Chiperoni Mountain, Portuguese East Africa. *Bull. Brit. Orn. Club* 70: 51.
Benson, C. W. (1960)   The birds of the Comoro Islands: results of the British Ornithologists' Union Centenary Expedition 1958. *Ibis* 103b: 5-106.
Benson, C. W. and Irwin, M. P. S. (1972)   The Thick-billed Cuckoo *Pacchycoccyx audeberti* (Schlegel) (Aves: Cuculidae). *Arnoldia (Rhod.)* 5(33).
Blot, J. (1985) Contribution à la connaissance de la biologie et de l'écologie de *Francolinus ochropectus* Dorst et Jouanin. *Alauda* 53: 244-256.
Bosser, J. (1982) Projet de constitution de réserves biologiques dans la domaine forestier à la Réunion. Rapport de mission. Paris: ORSTOM.
Bousquet, B. (1978)   Un parc de forêt dense en Afrique: le Parc National de Taï (Côte-d'Ivoire). *Bois et Forêts des Tropiques* no. 179: 28-46; no. 180: 26-37.
Bowden, C. G. R. (1986a)   Small mammal research in western Cameroon. Pp.196-200 in S. N. Stuart, ed. *Conservation of Cameroon montane forests.* Cambridge, U.K.: International Council for Bird Preservation.
Bowden, C. G. R. (1986b)   Records of other species of mammal from western Cameroon.   Pp. 201-203 in S. N. Stuart, ed. *Conservation of Cameroon montane forests.* Cambridge, U.K.: International Council for Bird Preservation.
Braithwaite, C. J. R. (1984)   Geology of the Seychelles. Pp. 17-38 in D. R. Stoddart, ed. *Biogeography and ecology of the Seychelles Islands.* The Hague: W. Junk (Monog. Biol. 55).
Bredero, J. T., Heemskerk, W. and Toxopeus, H. (1977)   Agriculture and livestock production in São Tomé and Príncipe (West Africa).   Wageningen: Foundation for Agricultural Plant Breeding (unpublished).
Brenan, J. P. M. (1978)   Some aspects of the phytogeography of Tropical Africa. *Ann. Missouri Bot. Garden* 65: 437-478.
Britton, P. L., ed. (1980)   *Birds of East Africa: their habitat, status and distribution.* Nairobi: East African Natural History Society.
Britton, P. L., Britton, H. A. and Coverdale, M. A. C. (1980)   The avifauna of Mrima Hill, south Kenya coast. *Scopus* 4: 73-78.
Britton, P. L. and Zimmerman, D. A. (1979)   The avifauna of Sokoke Forest, Kenya. *J. East Afr. Nat. Hist. Soc. and Natn. Mus.* no. 169.
Broadley, G. (1976)   The reptiles and amphibians of Chirinda Forest. *Rhodesia Science News* 10: 51-52.
Brosset, A. and Erard, C. (1986)   *Les oiseaux des régions forestières du nord-est du Gabon, 1. Ecologie et comportement des espèces.* Paris: Société Nationale de Protection de la Nature.
Brown, L. H. and Britton, P. L. (1980)   *The breeding seasons of East African birds.* Nairobi: East Africa Natural History Society.
Butynski, T. M. (1984)   Ecological survey of the Impenetrable (Bwindi) Forest, Uganda, and recommendations for its conservation and management.   New York Zoological Society, unpublished report to the Uganda government.
Butynski, T. M. (1985)   Primates and their conservation in the Impenetrable (Bwindi) Forest, Uganda. *Primate Conservation* 6: 68-72.
Butynski, T. M. (1986)   Probing the Impenetrable. *WWF Monthly Report,* July: 193-197.

de Campos, E. (1956) Modificação do ambiente das ilhas de S. Tomé e Príncipe. *Bol. Soc. Geog. Lisboa* 74 (4-6): 141-150.

Carter, M. F. (1987) Initial avifaunal survey of Sapo National Park, Liberia. A report to World Wildlife Fund International and Forestry Development Authority, Liberia.

Castroviejo Bolívar, J., Juste Balleste, J. and Castelo Alvarez, R. (1986) *Investigación y conservación de la naturaleza en Guinea Ecuatorial*. Madrid: Ministerio de Asuntos Exteriores.

Chapman, J, D. and White, F. (1970) *The evergreen forests of Malawi*. Oxford: Commonwealth Forestry Institute, University of Oxford.

Cheke, A. S. (1977) Rapport sur la distribution et la conservation du Tuit-tuit, oiseau rarissime de la Réunion. *Info-Nature* 15: 21-38.

Cheke, A. S. (1987a) The ecology of the surviving native landbirds of Réunion. Pp. 301-358 in A. W. Diamond, ed. *Studies of Mascarene Island birds*. Cambridge: Cambridge University Press.

Cheke, A. S. (1987b) The ecology of the smaller land-birds of Mauritius. Pp. 151-207 in A. W. Diamond, ed. *Studies of Mascarene Island birds*. Cambridge: Cambridge University Press.

Cheke, A. S. (1987c) An ecological history of the Mascarene Islands, with particular reference to extinctions and introductions of land vertebrates. Pp. 5-89 in A. W. Diamond, ed. *Studies of Mascarene Island birds*. Cambridge: Cambridge University Press.

Cheke, A. S. (1987d) The legacy of the dodo – conservation in Mauritius. *Oryx* 21: 29-36.

Chevalier, A. (1939a) La flore de la Somalie française et la forêt-relique du Mont Goudah. *C. R. Acad. Sci.* 209: 73-76.

Chevalier, A. (1939b) La Somalie française. Sa flore et ses productions végétales. *Rev. Bot. Appl. d'Agric. trop.* 19(209-210): 663-687.

Clancey, P. A. (1964) *The birds of Natal and Zululand*. Edinburgh and London: Oliver and Boyd.

Clarke, J. (1987) Introduction. Pp. 2-3 in Report of the Cambridge Bwindi Forest Study Group, August-October 1984. Unpublished.

Cloutier, A. and Dufresne, A. (1986) Parc National de Korup, plan de gestion préliminaire. Unpublished.

Coe, M. (1975) Mammalian ecological studies on Mount Nimba, Liberia. *Mammalia* 39: 523-587.

Coe, M. and Curry-Lindahl, K. (1965) Ecology of a mountain: first report on Liberian Nimba. *Oryx* 8: 177-184.

Cole, N. H. A. (1980) The Gola Forest in Sierra Leone: a remnant primary tropical rainforest in need of conservation. *Envir. Conserv.* 7: 33-40.

Collar, N. J. (1987) Red Data Books and national conservation strategies. *World Birdwatch* 9(2): 6-7.

Collar, N. J. and Andrew, P. (1988) *Birds to watch: the ICBP world checklist of threatened birds*. Cambridge, U.K.: International Council for Bird Preservation (Techn. Publ. 8).

Collar, N. J., Dee, T. J. and Goriup, P. D. (1987) La conservation de la nature à Madagascar: la perspective du CIPO. Pp. 97-108 in R. A. Mittermeier, L. H. Rakotovao, V. Randrianasolo, E. J. Sterling and D. Devitre, eds. *Priorités en matière de conservation des espèces à Madagascar*. Gland, Switzerland: IUCN/SSC Occ. Pap. 2.

Collar, N. J. and Stuart, S. N. (1985) *Threatened birds of Africa and related islands: the ICBP/IUCN Red Data Book*, part 1 (3rd edition). Cambridge, U.K.: International Council for Bird Preservation and International Union for Conservation of Nature and Natural Resources.

Collinet, J., Couturier, G., Guillaumet, J.-L., Kahn, F., Moreau, R. and Sangaré, Y. (1984) Le système cultural et ses contraintes. Pp. 113-184 in J.-L. Guillaumet, G. Couturier and H. Dosso, eds. *Recherche et aménagement en milieu forestier tropical humide: le Project Taï de Côte-d'Ivoire.* Paris: UNESCO (Notes techniques du MAB 15).

Collins, N. M. and Clifton, M. P. (1984) Threatened wildlife in the Taita Hills. *Swara* 7(5): 10-14.

Collins, N. M. and Morris, M. G. (1985) *Threatened swallowtail butterflies of the world: the IUCN Red Data Book.* Gland, Switzerland, and Cambridge, U.K.: International Union for Conservation of Nature and Natural Resources.

Colston, P. R. (1972) A new bulbul from southwestern Madagascar. *Ibis* 114: 89-92.

Colston, P. R. and Curry-Lindahl, K. (1986) *The birds of Mount Nimba, Liberia.* London: British Museum (Natural History).

Cords, M. (1982) A report on harmful exploitation of indigenous forest in Kakamega. Unpublished.

Cumming, D. H. M. and Jackson, P. (1984) *The status and conservation of Africa's elephants and rhinos.* Gland, Switzerland: International Union for Conservation of Nature and Natural Resources.

Cunningham-van Someren, G. R. (1982) Review of habitat status of some important biotic communities in Kenya. Unpublished.

Curry-Lindahl, K. (1969) *Report to the Government of Liberia on conservation, management and utilization of wildlife resources.* Morges, Switzerland: IUCN Publications (NS) Suppl. Pap. no. 24.

Davies, A. G. (1987) *The Gola Forest Reserves, Sierra Leone: wildlife conservation and forest management.* Gland, Switzerland, and Cambridge, U.K.: International Union for Conservation of Nature and Natural Resources.

Deans Cowan, W. (1882) Notes on the natural history of Madagascar. *Proc. Roy. Phys. Soc. Edinburgh* 7: 133-150.

Decker, B. S. (1987) The Tana River National Primate Reserve. *Swara* 10(4): 13-15.

Dee, T. J. (1986) *The endemic birds of Madagascar.* Cambridge, U.K.: International Council for Bird Preservation.

Diamond, A. W. and Fayad, V. C. (1979) Preliminary comparisons between the avifaunas of the North Nandi and Kakamega Forests. *Scopus* 3: 93-100.

Diamond, T. (1979) Kakamega: is there a way to stop the rot? *Swara* 2(1): 25-26.

Dixey, F. (1927) The Mlanje Mountains of Nyasaland. *Geogr. Rev.* 17: 611-626.

Dosso, H., Guillaumet, J. L. and Hadley, M. (1981) The Tai Project: land use problems in a tropical rain forest. *Ambio* 10: 120-125.

Doute, R., Ochanda, N. and Epp, H. (1981) A forest inventory of Kenya using remote sensing techniques. Nairobi: Kenya Rangeland Ecological Monitoring Unit, Ministry of Environment and Natural Resources, unpublished report.

Downer, E. R. and Redman, R. J. (1967) *Atlas of Uganda.* Second edition. [Kampala:] Department of Lands and Surveys, Uganda.

Dowsett, R. J. (1985) The conservation of tropical forest birds in central and southern Africa. Pp. 197-212 in A. W. Diamond and T. E. Lovejoy, eds. *Con-*

servation of tropical forest birds. Cambridge, U.K.: International Council for Bird Preservation (Techn. Publ. 4).

Dowsett, R. J. and Prigogine, A. (1974) The avifauna of the Marungu Highlands. *Hydrobiological survey of the Lake Bangweulu Luapula River Basin,* 19. Brussels: Cercle Hydrobiologique de Bruxelles.

Dowsett-Lemaire, F. and Dowsett, R. J. (in prep.). The evergreen forests of Malawi: their natural history and conservation status. Typescript.

Drapkin, J. (1987) History and management. Pp. 54-64 in S. L. Tetlow, ed. *Cambridge conservation study 1985: Taita Hills, Kenya.* Cambridge, U.K.: International Council for Bird Preservation (Study Report 19).

DS (1978) = Department of Surveys (1978) Republic of Malawi: maps illustrating development projects 1978/79-1980/81. Blantyre: Department of Surveys.

Duff-Mackay, A. (1980) Conservation status report No. 1: Amphibia. Nairobi: National Museums of Kenya.

Dufresne, A. and Cloutier, A. (1982) Rapport de mission IUCN/WWF/ Parcs Canada: Cameroun. Programme de conservation des forêts tropicales humides et des primates. IUCN/WWF Project 3053 (unpublished).

East, R. (1988) *Antelopes: global survey and regional action plans. Part 1: East and Northeast Africa.* Gland, Switzerland: International Union for Conservation of Nature and Natural Resources.

Edwards, I. (1985) Conservation of plants on Mulanje Mountain, Malawi. *Oryx* 19: 86-90.

Eisentraut, M. (1973) Die Wirbeltierfauna von Fernando Poo und Westkamerun. *Bonn. zool. Monogr.* 3.

Exell, A. W. (1944) *Catalogue of the vascular plants of S. Tomé (with Principe and Annobon).* London: Trustees of the British Museum.

Exell, A. W. (1952) The vegetation of the islands of the Gulf of Guinea. *Lejeunia* 16: 57-66.

Exell, A. W. (1973) Angiosperms of the islands of the Gulf of Guinea (Fernando Po, Príncipe, S. Tomé, and Annobon). *Bull. Brit. Mus. (Nat. Hist.) Bot.* 4(8): 325-411.

FDA/IUCN (1986) = Forestry Development Authority of the Republic of Liberia and the International Union for Conservation of Nature and Natural Resources (1986) Integrated management and development plan for Sapo National Park and surrounding areas in Liberia. Gland, Switzerland: IUCN (WWF/IUCN Project 3216) (unpublished).

FGU-Kronberg (1979) *Etat actuel des Parcs Nationaux de la Comoe et de Tai ainsi que de la Réserve d'Azagny et propositions visant à leur conservation et à leur développement aux fins de promotion du tourisme, 3: Parc National de Tai.* Eschborn: Deutsche Gesellschaft für Technische Zusammenarbeit.

Fox, J. E. D. (1968) Exploitation of the Gola Forest. *J. West Afr. Sci. Assoc.* 13: 185-210.

Fox, N., Fox, B. and Bailey, T. (1985) The predation ecology of the Mauritius Kestrel *(Falco punctatus).* Interim report (unpublished draft).

Friedmann, H. and Williams, J. G. (1971) The birds of the lowlands of Bwamba, Toro Province, Uganda. *Los Angeles Co. Mus. Contrib. Sci.* 211.

Gartlan, J. S. (1982a) The forests and primates of Ghana: prospects for protection and proposals for assistance. *Lab. Primate Newsletter* 21(1): 1-14.

Gartlan, J. S. (1982b) Forest conservation in Cameroon: the current situation. *IUCN/SSC Primate Specialist Group Newsletter* 2: 20.

Gartlan, J. S. and Agland, P. C. (undated [= 1981]) A proposal for a program of rain-forest conservation and national park development in Cameroon, west-central Africa. Presented to the Gulf Oil Corporation and Société Nationale Elf Acquitaine. World Wildlife Fund (unpublished).

Gartlan, J. S. (1986) The biological and historical importance of the Korup forest. Pp. 28-35 in S. Gartlan and H. Macleod, eds. *Proceedings of the workshop on Korup National Park.* Gland, Switzerland: World Wildlife Fund and International Union for Conservation of Nature and Natural Resources, project 3206.

Gartshore, M. E. (1986) The status of the montane herpetofauna of the Cameroon highlands. Pp. 204-240 in S. N. Stuart, ed. *Conservation of Cameroon montane forests.* Cambridge, U.K.: International Council for Bird Preservation.

Gatter, W. (1985) Ein neuer Bülbül aus Westafrika (Aves, Pycnonotidae). *J. Orn.* 126: 155-161.

Gbile, Z. O., Ola-Adams, B. A. and Soladoye, M. O. (1978) List of endangered species of the Nigerian flora. *Nigerian J. Forestry* 8: 14-20.

Glover, P. E. (1968) Report on an ecological survey of the proposed Shimba Hills National Reserve. Nairobi: East African Wildlife Society, unpublished report.

Godfrey, L. and Vuillaume-Randriamanantena, M. (1986) *Hapalemur simus*: endangered lemur once widespread. *Primate Conservation* 7: 92-96.

Goldsmith, B. (1976) The trees of Chirinda Forest. *Rhodesia Science News* 10: 41-50.

Griveaud, P. (1961) Un intéressant vestige forestier malgache. *Bull. Acad. Malgache* 39: 9-10.

Guillaumet, J.-L. (1976) The Ivory Coast Tai Forest Project: research plans, progress and prospects. *Nature and Resources* 12(2): 3-5.

Guillaumet, J.-L., Betsch, J.-M., Blanc, C., Morat, P., Peyrieras, A. and Paulian, R. (1975) Etude des écosystèmes montagnards dans la région malgache. III. Le Marojezy. IV. L'Itremo et l'Ibity. Géomorphologie, climatologie, faune et flore (Campagne RCP 225, 1971-1973). *Bull. Mus. Natn. Hist. Nat.* (Ser. 3, Ecol. gén.) 25 (no. 309): 29-67.

Guillaumet, J.-L. and Boesch, C. (1984) Le parc national et la protection de la nature. Pp. 207-216 in J.-L. Guillaumet, G. Couturier and H. Dosso, eds. *Recherche et aménagement en milieu forestier tropical humide: le Project Taï de Côte-d'Ivoire.* Paris: UNESCO (Notes techniques du MAB 15).

Guillaumet, J.-L., Kahn, F. and Léna, P. (1984) Présentation du projet. Pp. 17-34 in J.-L. Guillaumet, G. Couturier and H. Dosso, eds. *Recherche et aménagement en milieu forestier tropical humide: le Project Taï de Côte-d'Ivoire.* Paris: UNESCO (Notes techniques du MAB 15).

Günther, R. and Feiler, A. (1985) Die Vögel der Insel São Tomé. *Mitt. zool. Mus. Berlin* 61, suppl. *Ann. Orn.* 9: 3-28.

Hall, B. P. (1960) The faunistic importance of the scarp of Angola. *Ibis* 102: 420-442.

Hall, B. P. and Moreau, R. E. (1962) A study of the rare birds of Africa. *Bull. Brit. Mus. (Nat. Hist.) Zool.* 8: 313-378.

Hall, J. B. (1981) Ecological islands in south-eastern Nigeria. *Afr. J. Ecol.* 19: 55-72.

Hall, J. B. and Swaine, M. D. (1981) *Distribution and ecology of vascular plants in a tropical rain forest: forest vegetation in Ghana.* The Hague: W. Junk.

Halle, M. (1983) Timber pressure on last Ivory Coast forest. *WWF News* no. 22: 2.

Harcourt, A. H. (1981) Can Uganda's gorillas survive? – A survey of the Bwindi Forest Reserve. *Biol. Conserv.* 19: 269-282.

Hart, J. A., Hart, T. B. and Thomas, S. (1986) The Ituri Forest of Zaïre: primate diversity and prospects for conservation. *Primate Conservation* 7: 42-44.

Hawthorne, W. D. (1985) East African coastal forests: botanical values, human threats and conservation priorities. Unpublished paper (presented to the symposium "The scramble for resources: conservation in Africa 1884-1984", African Studies Centre, Cambridge, U.K., 19-20 April 1985).

Hazlewood, P. and Stotz, D. (1981) Draft environmental profile on United Republic of Cameroon. Tucson, Arizona: Arid Lands Information Center, Office of Arid Lands Studies. (National Park Service Contract no. CX-0001-0-0003 in cooperation with U.S. Man and the Biosphere Secretariat, Department of State, Washington D.C.; funded by AID, Office of Science and Technology under SA/TOA 1-77.)

Homewood, K. M. and Rodgers, W. A. (1981) A previously undescribed mangabey from southern Tanzania. *Internatn. J. Primatol.* 2: 47-55.

Horsten, F. (1982) Os parques nacionais e as outras zonas de protecção de natureza de Angola. Material de estudo para os técnicos e agentes de conservação da natureza no. 2. Luanda: Direcção Nacional da Conservação da Natureza, Ministério de Agricultura.

Howard, P. C. (1986a) Conservation of tropical forest wildlife in western Uganda (World Wildlife Fund Project 3235). Annual report, March 1986.

Howard, P. C. (1986b) Agricultural encroachment in the Semliki Forest Reserve, western Uganda. World Wildlife Fund and New York Zoological Society, unpublished report.

Howard, P. C. (1986c) Bwamba Natural Resources Development Project: an outline. Unpublished.

Howell, K. M. (1981) Pugu Forest Reserve: biological values and development. *Afr. J. Ecol.* 19: 73-81.

Hughes, F. M. R. (1984) A comment on the impact of development schemes on the floodplain forests of the Tana River of Kenya. *Geog. J.* 150: 230-244.

Hughes, F. (1987) Conflicting uses for forest resources in the lower Tana River basin of Kenya. Pp. 211-228 in D. Anderson and R. Grove, eds. *Conservation in Africa: people, policies and practice.* Cambridge: Cambridge University Press.

Hughes, F. M. R. (in press) The ecology of African floodplain forests in semi-arid and arid zones: a review. *J. Biogeog.* 14.

Huntley, B. J. (1965) A preliminary account of the Ngoye Forest Reserve, Zululand. *J. South Afr. Bot.* 31: 177-205.

Huntley, B. J. (1974a) Outlines of wildlife conservation in Angola. *J. Sn. Afr. Wildlife Mgmt. Assoc.* 4: 157-166.

Huntley, B. J. (1974b) Ecosystem conservation priorities in Angola. Unpublished.

Huntley, B. J. (1978) Ecosystem conservation in southern Africa. Pp. 1333-1384 in M. J. A. Werger and A. C. van Bruggen, eds. *Biogeography and ecology of southern Africa.* The Hague: W. Junk.

Hutterer, R. (1986) Diagnosen neuer Spitzmäuse aus Tanzania. *Bonn. zool. Beitr.* 37: 23-33.

Irwin, M. P. S. (1979) The Zimbabwe-Rhodesian and Moçambique highland avian endemics: their evolution and origins. *Honeyguide* no.99: 5-11.

Irwin, M. P. S. (1981) *The birds of Zimbabwe.* Salisbury, Zimbabwe: Quest Publishing.

IUCN (1972) *C. R. Conférence Internationale sur la Conservation de la Nature et de ses Ressources à Madagascar.* Morges: IUCN(NS) Doc. suppl. no. 36.

IUCN (1986) *An outline of the plant sites Red Data Book.* Kew, U.K.: International Union for Conservation of Nature and Natural Resources (Threatened Plants Unit).

IUCN/CMC (1986) = IUCN Conservation Monitoring Centre (1986) *1986 IUCN Red List of threatened animals.* Gland, Switzerland, and Cambridge, U.K.: International Union for Conservation of Nature and Natural Resources.

IUCN/UNEP (1987) *IUCN directory of Afrotropical protected areas.* Cambridge, U.K.: International Union for Conservation of Nature and Natural Resources.

Jaeger, P. and Adam, J. G. (1975) Les forêts de l'étage culminal du Nimba Libérien. *Adansonia* 2,15: 177-188.

Jenkins, M. ed. (1987) *Madagascar: an environmental profile.* Cambridge, U.K.: International Union for Conservation of Nature and Natural Resources.

Johansson, D. R. (1978) *Saintpaulias* in their natural environment with notes on their present status in Tanzania and Kenya. *Biol. Conserv.* 14: 45-62.

Johnston-Stewart, N. G. B. (1977) Birds of Thyolo District. *Nyala* 3: 67-96.

Johnston-Stewart, N. G. B. (1982) Evergreen forest birds in upper Thyolo. *Nyala* 8: 69-84.

Jones, P. J. and Tye, A. (1988) *A survey of the avifauna of São Tomé and Príncipe.* Cambridge, U.K.: International Council for Bird Preservation (Study Report 24).

Kalina, J. and Butynski, T. M. (1986) The Impenetrable Forest. *Animal Kingdom* 89(2): 51-58.

Keith, S. Forbes-Watson, A. D. and Turner D. A. (1974) The Madagascar Crested Ibis, a threatened species in an endemic and endangered avifauna. *Wilson Bull.* 86: 197-199.

Kelsey, M. G. (1986) Report on a visit to Nairobi and the Arabuko-Sokoke Forest, Dec. 1986. Unpublished.

Kelsey, M. G. and Langton, T. E. S. (1984) *The conservation of the Arabuko-Sokoke Forest, Kenya.* Cambridge, U.K.: International Council for Bird Preservation (Study Report 4).

King, W. B. (1978-1979) *Red Data Book, 2: Aves.* Second edition. Morges, Switzerland: International Union for Conservation of Nature and Natural Resources.

Kingdon, J. (1974a) *East African mammals. An atlas of evolution in Africa,* 2a. London and New York: Academic Press.

Kingdon, J. (1974b) *East African mammals. An atlas of evolution in Africa,* 2b. London and New York: Academic Press.

Kingdon, J. (1977) *East African mammals. An atlas of evolution in Africa,* 3a. London and New York: Academic Press.

Lains e Silva, H. (1958) Esboço da carta de aptidão agrícola de São Tomé e Príncipe. *Garcia de Orta* 6: 61-86.

Lamotte, M. (1983) The undermining of Mount Nimba. *Ambio* 12: 174-179.

Lamprey, H. F. (1975) *The distribution of protected areas in relation to the needs of biotic community conservation in eastern Africa.* Morges, Switzerland:

International Union for Conservation of Nature and Natural Resources (Occasional Paper no. 16).

Louette, M., Stevens, J., Bijnens, L. and Janssens, L. (1986) Comoro Islands endemic bird survey. International Council for Bird Preservation, final report (30 April 1986), unpublished. [Published in 1988 as *A survey of the endemic avifauna of the Comoro Islands* (ICBP Study Report 25).]

Lovett, J. C. (1985) An overview of the moist forest of Tanzania. Final report of the Tanzania Forest Habitat Evaluation Project. Tanzania National Scientific Research Council/World Wildlife Fund, unpublished report.

Lovett, J. and Lovett, J. (1985) Preliminary report of the first international Uzungwa expedition. Unpublished.

Lucas, G. and Synge, H. (1978) *The IUCN Plant Red Data Book.* Morges, Switzerland: International Union for Conservation of Nature and Natural Resources.

MacKinnon, J. and MacKinnon, K. (1986) *Review of the protected areas system in the Afrotropical realm.* Gland, Switzerland, and Cambridge, U.K.: International Union for Conservation of Nature and Natural Resources, with United Nations Environment Programme.

Macleod, H. M. (1987) *The conservation of Oku Mountain Forest, Cameroon.* Cambridge, U.K.: International Council for Bird Preservation (Study Report 15).

Malpas, R. (1980) Wildlife in Uganda 1980: a survey. A report to the Minister of Tourism and Wildlife, Uganda. Unpublished.

Mankoto ma Mbaelele (1984) Rôle de la forêt dans l'équilibre et quelques aspects de l'impact de la déforestation sur l'environnement. Pp. 197-220 in *Premier symposium sur la "Forêt: richesse nationale à préserver".* Kinshasa: Département de l'Environnement, Conservation de la Nature et Tourisme.

Mann, C. F. (1985) An avifaunal study in Kakamega Forest, Kenya, with particular reference to species diversity, weight and moult. *Ostrich* 56: 236-262.

Marsh, C. (1976) A management plan for the Tana River Game Reserve, Kenya. New York Zoological Society and University of Bristol, unpublished.

Marsh, C. (1986) A resurvey of Tana River primates and their habitat. *Primate Conservation* 7: 72-82.

Masterson, A. N. B. (1985) Notes from the Vumba. *Honeyguide* 31: 6-10.

McGuigan, C. (1987) Ornithology. Pp. 10-27 in S. L. Tetlow, ed. *Cambridge conservation study 1985: Taita Hills, Kenya.* Cambridge, U.K.: International Council for Bird Preservation (Study Report 19).

Merz, G. (1986) The status of the Forest Elephant *Loxodonta a. cyclotis* Matschie, 1900, in the Gola Forest Reserves, Sierra Leone. *Biol. Conserv.* 36: 83-94.

Merz, G. and Roth, H. H. (1984) Conservation of elephants in Sierra Leone, with special reference to the management of the Gola Forest complex. Final report on IUCN/WWF project no. 3039 (unpublished).

MC (1948) = Ministério das Colónias (1948) *Atlas de Portugal Ultramarino e das grandes viagens portuguesas de descòbrimento e expansão.* Lisboa: Junta das Missões Geográficas e de Investigações Coloniais.

Mitchell, T. (1988) Preliminary report of the Cambridge Ghana Rainforest Project 1988. Unpublished.

Mittermeier, R. A. (in prep.) *An action plan for the conservation of biological diversity in Madagascar.* Gland, Switzerland: IUCN Species Survival Commission.

MOD (DOS) (1978) Map of Mahé, series Y851 (DOS 204), edition 3-DOS 1978, 1:10,000. Republic of Seychelles.

Moll, E. J. (1978) A plea for Ngoye Forest. *Trees in South Africa* 30: 63-71.

Monfort, A. (1983) Nyungwe Forest, Rwanda. *Swara* 6(6): 22.

Monod, T. (1960) Notes botaniques sur les îles de São Tomé et de Príncipe. *Bull. Inst. Franc. Afr. Noire* 22 (ser. A): 19-83.

Moreau, R. E. (1935) A synecological study of Usambara, Tanganyika Territory, with particular reference to birds. *J. Ecol.* 23: 1-43.

Moreau, R. E. (1966) *The bird faunas of Africa and its islands.* London: Academic Press.

Nicoll, M. and Langrand, O. (1986a) Conservation et utilisation rationelle des écosystèmes forestiers du Gabon, project 3247. Gland, Switzerland: World Wide Fund for Nature, and International Union for Conservation of Nature and Natural Resources, unpublished report.

Nicoll, M. E. and Langrand, O. (1986b) Report on the first phase of WWF-protected areas programme in Madagascar. Unpublished.

Numbem, S. T. (1987) Climate, geology, soils and drainage pattern of Mount Oku. Pp. 44-52 in H. M. Macleod, *The conservation of Oku Mountain Forest, Cameroon.* Cambridge, U.K.: International Council for Bird Preservation (Study Report 15).

Nussbaum, R. A. (1984) Amphibians of the Seychelles. Pp. 379-415 in D. R. Stoddart, ed. *Biogeography and ecology of the Seychelles Islands.* The Hague: W. Junk (Monog. Biol. 55).

Oates, J. F. (1986) *Action plan for African primate conservation: 1986-90.* New York: IUCN/SSC Primate Specialist Group.

O'Connor, S., Pidgeon, M. and Randria, Z. (1985) A conservation program for the Andohahela Reserve (Reserve Naturalle No. 11). Unpublished.

van Orsdol, K. G. (1983a) Survey report on the Semliki (Bwamba) Forest Reserve of western Uganda. Unpublished.

van Orsdol, K. G. (1983b) The status of Kibale Forest Reserve of western Uganda and recommendations for its conservation and management. Unpublished.

van Orsdol, K. G. (1986) Agricultural encroachment in Uganda's Kibale Forest. *Oryx* 20: 115-117.

Pakenham, R. H. W. (1979) *The birds of Zanzibar and Pemba.* London: British Ornithologists' Union (Check-list 2).

Phillipson, J. R. (1978) Wildlife conservation and management in Sierra Leone. Special report to MAF, Freetown (unpublished).

Pinto, A. A. da R. (1959) Um esbôço da avifauna sedentária da região da Gorongoza, Moçambique. *Proc. I Pan-Afr. orn. Congr.* (*Ostrich* suppl.3): 98-125.

Pócs, T. (1974) Bioclimatic studies in the Uluguru Mountains (Tanzania, East Africa) I. *Act. Bot. Acad. Sci. Hung.* 20: 115-135.

Pócs, T. (1976a) Bioclimatic studies in the Uluguru Mountains (Tanzania, East Africa) II. Correlations between orography, climate and vegetation. *Act. Bot. Acad. Sci. Hung.* 22: 163-183.

Pócs, T. (1976b) Vegetation mapping in the Uluguru Mountains (Tanzania, East Africa). *Boissiera* 24: 477-498.

Prigogine, A. (1978) Note sur les petits indicateurs de la Forêt de Kakamega. *Gerfaut* 68: 87-89.

Prigogine, A. (1980) The altitudinal distribution of the avifauna in the Itombwe Forest (Zaïre). *Proc. IV Pan-Afr. Orn. Congr.*: 169-184.

Prigogine, A. (1985) Conservation of the avifauna of the forests of the Albertine Rift. Pp. 277-295 in A. W. Diamond and T. E. Lovejoy, eds. *Conservation of tropical forest birds.* Cambridge, U.K.: International Council for Bird Preservation (Techn. Publ. 4).

Procter, J. (1984) Vegetation of the granitic islands of the Seychelles. Pp. 193-207 in D. R. Stoddart, ed. *Biogeography and ecology of the Seychelles Islands.* The Hague: W. Junk (Monog. Biol. 55).

Procter, J. and Salm, R. (1974) Conservation in Mauritius 1974. IUCN/ WWF consultancy report for Government of Mauritius. Unpublished.

Racey, P. A. and Nicoll, M. E. (1984) Mammals of the Seychelles. Pp. 607-626 in D. R. Stoddart, ed. *Biogeography and ecology of the Seychelles Islands.* The Hague: W. Junk (Monog. Biol. 55).

Rahm, U. (1954) La Côte d'Ivoire, Centre de Recherches tropicales. *Acta Tropica* 11(3): 1-73.

Rahm, U. (1973) *Propositions pour la création du Parc national ivoirien de Taï.* Morges, Switzerland: IUCN Occ. Pap. no. 3.

Rand, A. L. (1936) The distribution and habits of Madagascar birds. *Bull. Amer. Mus. Nat. Hist.* 72: 143-499.

Rathbun, G. B. (1979) *Rhynchocyon chrysopygus. Mammalian Species* 117.

Robertson, F. (1986) A study of the conservation status of Botanical Reserves in Zimbabwe. *Zimbabwe Science News* 20: 102-106.

Robinson, P. T. (undated) The proposed Sarpo [sic] National Park in Liberia: a field survey of prospects and problems. *Natn. Geogr. Soc. Res. Rep.* 21: 425-435.

Robinson, P. T. (1982a) Sapo Forest to be Liberia's first national park. *WWF Monthly Reports*, October: 285-288.

Robinson, P. T. (1982b) The proposed Sarpo [sic] National Park in Liberia: a field survey of prospects and problems. Unpublished.

Robinson, P. T. and Peal, A. (1981) Liberia's wildlife – the time for decision. *Zoonooz* 54(10): 7-21.

Rodgers, W. A. (1981) The distribution and conservation status of colobus monkeys in Tanzania. *Primates* 22: 33-45.

Rodgers, W. A., Hall, J. B., Mwasumbi, L. B., Griffiths, C. J. and Vollesen, K. (1983) The conservation values and status of Kimboza Forest Reserve, Tanzania. University of Dar es Salaam, Forest Conservation Working Group, unpublished report.

Rodgers, W. A. and Homewood, K. M. (1982a) Species richness and endemism in the Usambara mountain forests, Tanzania. *Biol. J. Linn. Soc.* 18: 197-242.

Rodgers, W. A. and Homewood, K. M. (1982b) Biological values and conservation prospects for the forests and primate populations of the Uzungwa Mountains, Tanzania. *Biol. Conserv.* 24: 285-304.

Rodgers, W. A., Homewood, K. M. and Hall, J. B. (1979) An ecological survey of Magombera Forest Reserve, Kilombero District, Tanzania. Dar es Salaam, unpublished report.

Ross, K. (1981) Shimba Hills Reserve land use study, final report: vegetation and land use changes in the Shimba Hills and its significance to the ecology of the large herbivores. Nairobi: EcoSystems Ltd.

Rodgers, W. A., Homewood, K. M. and Hall, J. B. (1980) The railway and a rare colobus monkey. *Oryx* 15: 491-495.

Roth, H. H. (1985) We all want the trees: resource conflict in the Tai National Park, Ivory Coast. Pp. 127-129 in J. A. McNeely and K. R. Miller, eds. *National parks, conservation, and development: the role of protected areas in sustaining society.* Washington, D.C.: Smithsonian Institution Press.

Rowell, T. (1982) Kakamega Forest. *Swara* 5(2): 8-9.

Scharff, N., Stoltze, M. and Jensen, F. P. (1981) The Uluguru Mts., Tanzania. Report of a study-tour, 1981. Unpublished.

Schiøtz, A. (1981) The amphibia in the forested basement hills of Tanzania: a biogeographical indicator group. *Afr. J. Ecol.* 19: 205-208.

Sidle, J. G. and Lawson, D. (1986) Conservation of okapi in the Ituri Forest. Report on Phase 1, August-October 1986. Tabazaire and World Wide Fund for Nature. Unpublished.

Skorupa, J. P. and Kasenene, J. M. (1984) Tropical forest management: can rates of natural treefalls help guide us? *Oryx* 18: 96-101.

Smithers, R. (1976) Mammals of the Chirinda Forest. *Rhodesia Science News* 10: 62-63.

Smithers, R. H. N. (1983) *The mammals of the southern African sub-region.* Pretoria: University of Pretoria.

Strahm, W. (in prep.) *Mauritius plant Red Data Book.* Gland, Switzerland: International Union for Conservation of Nature and Natural Resources.

Stresemann, E. (1926) *Copsychus albospecularis* (Eydoux & Gervais). (Mutationsstudien XXIV). *Orn. Monatsber.* 34: 38-41.

Struhsaker, T. and Leland, L. (1979) Kibale: an inheritance still preserved. *Swara* 2(1): 18, 23-24.

Stuart, S. N. (1983) Biogeographical and ecological aspects of forest bird communities in eastern Tanzania. University of Cambridge, unpublished Ph.D. dissertation.

Stuart, S. N. (1985) Rare forest birds and their conservation in eastern Africa. Pp. 187-196 in A. W. Diamond and T. E. Lovejoy, eds. *Conservation of tropical forest birds.* Cambridge, U.K.: International Council for Bird Preservation (Techn. Publ. 4).

Stuart, S. N., ed. (1986a) *Conservation of Cameroon montane forests.* Cambridge, U.K.: International Council for Bird Preservation.

Stuart, S. N. (1986b) Usambara Mountains. *World Birdwatch* 8(3): 8-9.

Stuart, S. N. and Collar, N. J. (in press) Birds at risk in Africa and related islands: the causes of their rarity and decline. *Proc. VI Pan-Afr. orn. Congr.*

Stuart, S. N. and Jensen, F. P. (1985) The avifauna of the Uluguru Mountains, Tanzania. *Gerfaut* 75: 155-197.

Stuart, S. N. and van der Willigen, T. A., eds. (1978) Report of the Cambridge Ecological Expedition to Tanzania 1978. Unpublished.

Stubbs, D. (1988) The Itombwe Mountains, eastern Zaire: feasibility assessment for establishing a new African mountain forest conservation project. Unpublished report for the Fauna and Flora Preservation Society.

Swynnerton, C. F. M. (1907) On the birds of Gazaland, Southern Rhodesia. *Ibis* (9)1: 30-74.

Tattersall, I. (1986) Notes on the distribution and taxonomic status of some subspecies of *Propithecus* in Madagascar. *Folia primatol.* 46: 51-63.

Taylor, I. R. and Macdonald, M. A. (1978) The birds of Bia National Park, Ghana. *Bull. Nigerian Orn. Soc.* 14(45): 36-41.

Taylor, M. E. (1986) Aspects on the biology of the four-toed mongoose *Bdeogale crassicauda.* *Cimbebasia* Ser. A, 8: 187-193.

Taylor, M. E. (1986) *Bdeogale crassicauda. Mammalian Species* 294.

Tetlow, S. (1987) Habitat survey. Pp. 37-53 in S. L. Tetlow, ed. *Cambridge conservation study 1985: Taita Hills, Kenya.* Cambridge, U.K.: International Council for Bird Preservation (Study Report 19).

The Times atlas to the world (1986) Comprehensive (seventh) edition. London: Times Books.

Thiollay, J.-M. (1985a) The birds of Ivory Coast. *Malimbus* 7: 1-59.

Thiollay, J.-M. (1985b) The West African forest avifauna: a review. Pp. 171-186 in A. W. Diamond and T. E. Lovejoy, eds. *Conservation of tropical forest birds.* Cambridge, U.K.: International Council for Bird Preservation (Techn. Publ. 4).

Thomas, D. W. (1986a) Vegetation in the montane forests of Cameroon. Pp. 20-27 in S. N. Stuart, ed. *Conservation of Cameroon montane forests.* Cambridge, U.K.: International Council for Bird Preservation.

Thomas, D. W. (1986b) The botanical uniqueness of Korup and its implications for ecological research. Pp. 36-40 in S. Gartlan and H. Macleod, eds. *Proceedings of the workshop on Korup National Park.* Gland, Switzerland: World Wildlife Fund and International Union for Conservation of Nature and Natural Resources, project 3206.

Thomas, D. W. (1987) Vegetation of Mount Oku. Pp. 54-56 in H. M. Macleod, *The conservation of Oku Mountain Forest, Cameroon.* Cambridge, U.K.: International Council for Bird Preservation (Study Report 15).

Tinley, K. L. (undated a) Sketch of Gorongosa National Park, Moçambique. Pp. 162-172 in *Proceedings [of a] symposium on nature conservation as a form of land use,* Gorongosa National Park, Moçambique, 13-17 September 1971. Pretoria: South African Commission for the Conservation and Utilization of the Soil (SARCCUS).

Tinley, K. L. (undated b) Determinants of coastal conservation: dynamics and diversity of the environment as exemplified by the Moçambique coast. Pp. 125-153 in *Proceedings [of a] symposium on nature conservation as a form of land use,* Gorongosa National Park, Moçambique, 13-17 September 1971. Pretoria: South African Commission for the Conservation and Utilization of the Soil (SARCCUS).

Tuboku-Metzger, D. (1983) Forest exploitation in Sierra Leone: a tale of devastation. *Ecologist* 13: 239-241.

Tye, H. (1986) Geology and landforms in the highlands of western Cameroon. Pp. 15-17 in S. N. Stuart, ed. *Conservation of Cameroon montane forests.* Cambridge, U.K.: International Council for Bird Preservation.

Vayssière, P. and Chédeville, E. (1960) La Réserve Naturelle du Mont Goda, Côte française des Somalis. *C. R. Soc. Biogéogr.* 27(321): 10-11.

Verschuren, J. (1975) Wildlife in Zaïre. *Oryx* 13: 149-163.

Verschuren, J. (1982) Hope for Liberia. *Oryx* 16: 421-427.

Verschuren, J. (1983) Conservation of tropical rainforest in Liberia: recommendations for wildlife conservation and national parks. Gland, Switzerland: International Union for Conservation of Nature and Natural Resources/World Wildlife Fund (unpublished).

Vesey-FitzGerald, L. D. E. F. (1940) On the vegetation of the Seychelles. *J. Ecol.* 28: 465-483.

Vincent, J. (1933) The Namuli Mountains, Portuguese East Africa. *Geogr. J.* 81: 314-327.

Vincent, J. (1933-1934) The birds of Northern Portuguese East Africa. Compris-
ing a list of, and observations on, the collections made during the British
Museum Expedition of 1931-32. – Parts I and II. *Ibis* (13)3: 611-652; (13)4:
126-160.
Walsh, R. D. (1984) Climate of the Seychelles. Pp. 39-62 in D. R. Stoddart,
ed. *Biogeography and ecology of the Seychelles Islands*. The Hague: W. Junk
(Monog. Biol. 55).
Weber, A. W. (1987) Socioecologic factors in the conservation of Afromontane
forest reserves. Pp. 205-229 in C. W. Marsh and R. A. Mittermeier, eds.
Primate conservation in the tropical rain forest. New York: Alan R. Liss., Inc.
(Monographs in Primatology, 9).
Weber, B. and Vedder, A. (1984) Forest conservation in Rwanda and Burundi.
Swara 7(6): 32-35.
Welch, G. R. and Welch, H. J. (1984) Djibouti Expedition March 1984. A
preliminary survey of *Francolinus ochropectus* and the birdlife of the country.
Unpublished.
Welch, G. R. and Welch, H. J. (1986) Djibouti II Autumn '85. Unpublished.
Welch, G., Welch, H., Denton, M. and Cogilan, S. (1986) Djibouti II preliminary
report, 9 October – 3 December 1985. *WPA News* 12: 24-27.
Wells, S. M., Pyle, R. M. and Collins, N. M. (1983) *The IUCN invertebrate red
data book*. Gland, Switzerland: International Union for Conservation of Nature
and Natural Resources.
White, F. (1983) *The vegetation of Africa*. Paris: United Nations Educational,
Scientific and Cultural Organisation.
Williams, J. G. (1956) The re-discovery of *Warsanglia johannis*. *Ibis* 98:
531-532.
van der Willigen, T. A. and Lovett, J. A., eds. (1981) Report of the Oxford
Expedition to Tanzania 1979. Unpublished.
Wilson, J. D., ed. (1987) The status and conservation of the montane forest
avifauna of Mount Oku, Cameroon. Cambridge, U.K.: International Council
for Bird Preservation, unpublished.
Wilson, J. R. (1981) Comments upon the ecology and conservation of the
Seychelles Scops Owl (*Otus insularis*). Unpublished.
Zimmerman, D. A. (1972) The avifauna of the Kakamega Forest, western Kenya,
including a bird population study. *Bull. Amer. Mus. Nat. Hist.* 149: 255-339.